OPERATION MONGOOSE:

Prelude of a Direct Invasion on Cuba

D1809801

OPERATION MONGOOSE:
Prelude of a Direct Invasion on Cuba

Jacinto Valdés - Dapena

Translated by
Ornán José Batista Peña

Editorial Capitán San Luis
Havana, 2004

Original title in Spanish: *Operación Mangosta: Preludio de la invasión directa a Cuba*
Editing: Josefina Ezpeleta Laplace / Interior design: Osvaldo Valdés / Cover design: Francisco Masvidal Gómez / Composition: Norma Ramírez Vega

© 2004, Jacinto Valdés-Dapena Vivanco
© 2004, Ornán José Batista Peña
© 2004, Editorial Capitán San Luis

ISBN: 959-211-259-2

Editorial Capitán San Luis
Ave. 25 No. 3406, entre 34 y 36, Playa,
Ciudad de La Habana, Cuba

All rights reserved. The reproduction of this work, including the cover design, transmitted in any manner, or means, in whole or in part, is strictly prohibited without prior written consent of the Publishing House.

CONTENTS

CHAPTER I. A Necessary Introduction

The battle of Bay of Pigs not only meant the first military defeat in the history of the United States, but also it reflected other transcendental aspects. The Cuban socialism, proclaimed hours before the invasion, had broken the myth of geographical fatalism, questioning topicality and validity of the Monroe Doctrine' postulates in the middle of the 20th century and the core of it: The Manifest Destiny.

The legend on the CIA infallibility, elaborated with precise accuracy by U.S. propaganda centers, vanished in the Cuban landscape in April 1961. In the record time of seventy-two hours the heroism of the whole country was opening a new phase in the inter-American relations. The Lenin thesis, vehemently defended by Ho Chi Minh in the '20s, concerning the relation between struggles for national liberation and socialism, was present in Our America, integrated to the popular, anti-imperialistic and nationalistic ideary of the Cuban Revolution, clearly expressed in José Martí's work.

After the Bay of Pigs, John F. Kennedy administration was immediately before the essential dilemma that would characterize U.S.-Cuba relations to the present: what policy to be designed, and what strategy to be followed. The administration could choose between two variants. The former one corresponded to an objective and pragmatic analysis—while rational—that permitted the assessment of the truly character, essence and projections of the Cuban Revolution, while a political and autochthonous process, not derived from the Cold War. Thus, ways, forms, and methods aimed at establishing a communication and a dialog with Cuba were to be examined.

The latter variant consisted in insisting to destroy the Revolution with all available resources. Kennedy did not hesitate and opted for counterrevolutionary violence. It is important to identify, in their general features, the focuses that provoked this decision, the ones that are expressed in the following aspects: Cuba was perceived from the perspective of the U.S. national security and represented a threat for that nation. On April 20, 1961, Kennedy stated:

> . . . Should it ever appear that the inter-American doctrine of non-interference merely conceals or excuses a policy of non-action—if the nations of this Hemisphere should fail to meet their commitments against outside communist penetration—then I want it clearly understood that this Government will not hesitate in meeting its primary obligations, which are the security of our Nation.[1]

The national interests of the United States required subordinating activity of the counterrevolution to the guidelines of the Washington policy on the Island.

In its strategy against socialism, particularly the movements of national liberation, the United States gave high importance to special operations. It was not by chance that it gave top priority to operations of green berets, created the Peace Corps, improved advisory to police corps in Latin America, and sponsored operations of political and ideological diversion.

In a meeting with specialists of the U.S. intelligence community, John F. Kennedy exposed his view concerning subversive actions:

> As military means become more lethal, which an increasing number of nations have access to them, subversive war, guerrilla warfare and other forms of struggle acquire higher significance. As thermonuclear weapons are more powerful, and there are fewer possibilities for their use, subversive operations play an increasing relevant role.[2]

1. U.S. Department of State, "Memorandum From the Acting Assistant Secretary of State for Inter-American Affairs (Coerr) to Secretary of State Rusk," in *Foreign Relations of the United States, 1961-1963,* Volume X, *Cuba 1961-1962* (Washington: U.S. Printing Office, 1997), 308.
2. Charisius, Albrecht and Julius Mader. *Nicht Länger Geheim* (Berlin: Deutscher Militärverlag, 1969).

The principle of the flexible response announced by Kennedy as the core of his project of foreign policy comprised:
- Conjugation of political, social and economic measures expressed in reformist programs;
- Formulation of active and reactive diplomacy;
- Development of operations for political and ideological diversion;
- Outbreak of local military conflicts to counteract activity of revolutionary movements.

It was, thus, exposed what would be subsequently called as low-intensity conflict, whose first trial was undertaken against Cuba after the Bay of Pigs, and which would be present in the U.S. policy towards Latin America and the Caribbean to the present.

CUBA STUDY GROUP OF MAXWELL TAYLOR. DIRECTIVES OF THE NATIONAL SECURITY COUNCIL. VIEWS OF KENNEDY'S ADVISORS

Shortly after the Bay of Pigs failure, president Kennedy gave Gen. Maxwell Taylor the mission of describing, explaining, and concluding on the causes that determined the disaster of Operation Pluto. Taylor's appointment was not a mere chance; it was the signal of Pentagon presence as a very important force in new subversive plans that were to be shaped on Cuba.

President Kennedy's instructions to Taylor, contained in an April 22, 1961 letter, were:

"To take a close look at all our practices and programs in the areas of military and paramilitary, guerrilla and anti-guerrilla activities which fall short of outright war. I believe we need to strengthen our work in this area. In the course of your study, I hope you will give special attention to the lessons which can be learned from recent events in Cuba."[3]

That same day, the first meeting of the General Taylor's Cuba Study Group for investigations on covert operations on Cuba developed by the

3. U.S. Department of State, "Memorandum for the Record," in *Foreign Relations of the United States, 1961-1963*, Volume X, *Cuba 1961-1962* (Washington: U.S. Printing Office, 1997), 318.

CIA, was held. It is important to mention its members, because it was made up by those who had had direct responsibilities in the execution of the Operation Pluto and by those who, subsequently, took the direction of the Operation Mongoose in 1962.

PARTICIPANTS

Study Group Members
General Maxwell Taylor
Attorney General Robert Kennedy
Admiral Arleigh Burke
Allen W. Dulles

Department of Defense
Major General David W. Gray
Colonel C. W. Shuler
Commander Mitchell

CIA Personnel
General C. P. Cabell
C. Tracy Barnes
Colonel J. C. King
Jacob D. Esterline
[*Name not declassified*]
Colonel Jack Hawkins[4]

In this working group, Richard Bissell, Chief of the CIA clandestine services, main architect of the Operation Pluto and one of the founders of the Central Intelligence Agency does not appear.

Analysis of points approached in this meeting gives much light on covert operations on Cuba, developed by the CIA in fulfillment of guidelines of foreign policy of the U.S. Government.

Colonel King (Chief of the CIA Western Hemisphere Division, to which the operational working group on Cuba was subordinated then) explained that by late 1958, the CIA undertook two attempts for preventing the revolutionary forces headed by Fidel Castro from taking the political power in Cuba. The first attempt was in November 1958 when

4. Ibid., 318-319.

the CIA contacted Justo Carrillo, of the Montecristi Group, to forge a plan that would impede the victory of the Rebel Army and displace Fidel Castro as the main leader of the revolutionary movement that faced the tyranny. The second attempt was to take place in December of that same year: The former U.S. ambassador in Brazil and Peru, William Pawley, supported by the Chief of the CIA station in Havana, contacted Batista and proposed him the creation of a Junta which he would give the power to.

In the meeting, a CIA specialist, not identified, explained that on September 21, 1959, he took the responsibility to plan potential actions of the CIA in contingency situations that might develop in Latin America. Most Central American countries (Guatemala, Nicaragua, Honduras, and El Salvador) were identified as potential contingency problems due to their governments lack of stability. Haiti and Santo Domingo were objectives of top priority. In South America, Paraguay, Bolivia, and Argentina were included among the countries that required to be studied.

Cuba was the objective number one for contingency planning. It was also considered that from the United States perspective, the Cuban situation continued worsening, and in December 1959 it was made the decision that the CIA needed to urgently consider the activation of two programs:

1. Selection, recruitment and careful assessment (including medical, psychological, psychiatric, and polygraph aspects) of about thirty-five Cubans, preferably with prior military experience, for intensive training program to make them be instructors in different paramilitary specialties (including leadership, sabotage, communications, etc.).

2. Undertake training of Cuban recruits, in a clandestine way, to be organized in small teams, similar to the concept of U.S. special forces, and to infiltrate them as communication agents in areas of Cuba where opposition centers were identified requiring specialized training, leadership and military insurance.

Jacob D. Esterline, one of the chiefs of the CIA Operational Group working on Cuba, made an analysis of the Cuban Task Force. This Task Force had been organized to undertake actions on Cuba, and steps that led to the report presented to president Eisenhower on March 14, 1960, which was the first authorization for mounting an operation aimed at overthrowing the Cuban Revolutionary Government.

Specialists of the CIA confirmed that the plan on Cuba was conceived with four main directions: (1) creation of political opposition;

11

(2) transmission means on Cuba; (3) creation of a paramilitary force outside Cuba, demanding talents of leaders, and (4) covert intelligence and actions from within Cuba.

From consulted information, it is obvious that already in the 1960 fall, the CIA recognized that its original plans conceived in the Operation Pluto were condemned to fail, so the concept of paramilitary force was interpreted now in Assault Brigade (force of military invasion). In operational terms this decision expresses a malfunction, while the covert operation became an overt operation.

Willing to intensify subversive action on Cuba, and in the middle of deliberations of the Study Group on Cuba concerning the causes of the fiasco of the Bay of Pigs and formulation of political proposals, the U.S. Government draws, in the meantime, guidelines aimed at undermining socialism in Cuba. A level of integration in political, military, economic, diplomatic, intelligence and propaganda factors characterizes these guidelines. All would be framed into the strategy to run out and destroy Cuba attacking all flanks; it was the Kennedys *Blitzkrieg* who had placed the Cuban issue in the center of the United States policy towards Latin America.

The May 4, 1961 memorandum of action No. 2413 of the National Security Council (NSC) contains the principal directions of subversion and terrorism strategies designed for the rest of 1961. The president would personally be in charge to give the relevant instructions.

The elements which characterize this strategy are expressed in the following indications, established by the NSC:

a) Agreed that U.S. policy towards Cuba should aim at the downfall of Castro, and . . . the matter should be reviewed . . . with a view of further actions.

b) Agreed that the United States should not undertake a military intervention in Cuba now, but should do nothing that would foreclose the possibility of military intervention in the future.[5]

On May Day 1961, Robert McNamara, Secretary of Defense of the United States had sent the chiefs of the JCS the contingency plan for Cuba. The content of this comprised:

5. U.S. Department of State, "Record of Action at the 438th Meeting of the National Security Council, in *Foreign Relations of the United States, 1961-1963*, Volume X, *Cuba 1961-1962* (Washington: U.S. Government Printing Office, 1997), 482.

- Invasion project of U.S. troops in Cuba.
- The use of 60,000 ground troops, but sea and aerial units.
- Preparations will be undertaken within a twenty-five-day term.
- The objective of the plan was to occupy the Island in eight days, even though it was considered that the Cuban Revolutionary Armed Forces (FAR) would fight guerrilla warfare against invaders in Oriente and the Escambray mountains.

c) Agreed that the United States should not impose a naval blockade or attempt an air war against Cuba. . . .

d) Noted the importance the President attaches to obtaining timely and adequate intelligence as to Cuban military capabilities, especially the enhancement of such capabilities by Sino-Soviet Bloc military assistance, so that U.S. capabilities for possible intervention may be maintained at an adequate level.

e) Noted the importance the President attaches to publication in the Free World press of terrorist actions of the Castro regime, and to possible political action to end the current terror.

f) Noted the President's direction that the Central Intelligence Agency, with other departments, should make a detailed study of possible weaknesses and vulnerabilities in the elements, which exert control in Cuba today.

g) Agreed that relations with the Revolutionary Council should be improved and made more open, and while it cannot be recognized as a government-in-exile, support should be given to it insofar as it continues to represent substantial Cuban sentiment.

h) Agreed that no separate Cuban military force should be organ-   ized in the United States, but that Cuban nationals would be encouraged to enlist in the U.S. armed forces under plans to be developed by the Secretary of Defense. . . .

j) Agreed not to impose an immediate trade embargo on Cuba. The Secretary of State agreed to send to the President an analysis of the effects of the U.S. embargo on trade with Cuba in relation to the Battle Act. It was agreed that when an embargo is imposed, it should be as complete as possible, with certain exceptions for . . . distributions of drugs.

k) Agreed that the United States should at once initiate negotiation to enlarge the willingness of other American states to join in bilateral, multilateral and OAS arrangements against Castro, such as (1) breaking diplomatic relations with Cuba; (2) controlling

13

subversive activities of Cuban agents; (3) preventing arm shipments to Castro; (4) limiting economic relations with Cuba; (5) creating a Caribbean security force; (6) initiating naval patrol to prevent Cuban invasion of other states in the Caribbean; (7) denunciation of Castro as agent of international communism by all nations of this hemisphere.

l) Agreed that the Alliance for Progress should be strengthened by such measures as (1) rapid implementation of selected social development projects; (2) acceleration of implementation of other Latin American aid; and (3) provision of additional resources for Latin American economic and social development, including consideration of a supplemental appropriation for development loans of the order of $200 - $400 million.

m) Agreed that the U.S. Information Agency would expand its existing program in Latin America, but not initiate electronic warfare against the Castro regime; means of propaganda should be made available to non-U.S. groups.[6]

n) Agreed that U.S. military officers, under general guidance to be prepared by the Department of State, would discuss the Castro threat to all Latin America with Latin American officers.

o) Agreed that the Secretary of State should prepare a report on possible judicial basis for effective anticommunist action.[7]

An important objective of propaganda campaigns on which the U.S. administration insists by the late first half of 1961 is in relation with the presentation of a new public image of the Cuban Revolution to the world. In this sense, the methods proposed by the advisors of national security intended to reveal, according to them, the character of the Cuban Revolution as a "betrayed revolution" and to show a progressive image of the Cuban Revolutionary Council (CRC) and its political will to save Cuba from communism.

The intention to present other image of Cuba was influenced by revealed results in a Gallup Poll, according to which 65.4% of the American people were against the armed intervention and just the 44.1% favored the indirect assistance of the counterrevolution.

---

6. That is, counterrevolutionary emigration groups.
7. U.S. Department of State, "Record of Action at the 438th Meeting of the National Security Council, in *Foreign Relations of the United States, 1961-1963*, Volume X, *Cuba 1961-1962* (Washington: U.S. Government Printing Office, 1997), 482-483.

On June 13, 1961, the Cuba Study Group submitted the U.S. president the report concerning the Operation Pluto.[8]

When interpreting this report, the following focuses are deduced and concluded:

1. The Operation Pluto in its character and essence did not correspond with the concept of covert operation as this is defined by the NSC of the United States.

2. The Central Intelligence Agency wrongly estimated the magnitude the operation might assume out of the operational context. The report expressed:

By about November 1960, the impossibility of running Zapata as a covert operation under CIA should have been recognized and the situation reviewed. The subsequent decision might then have been made to limit the efforts to attain covertness to the degree and nature of U.S. participation, and to assign responsibility for the amphibious operation to the Department of Defense. In this case, the CIA would have assisted in concealing the participation of Defense. Failing such a reorientation, the project should have been abandoned.[9]

3. The principle of co-operation and coordination that rules the U.S. Government policy was openly violated. Thus, it is exposed in the report:

Once the need of the operation was established, its success should have had the primary consideration of all agencies in the Government. Operational restrictions designed to protect its covert character should have been accepted only if did not impair the chance of success. As it was, the leaders of the operation were obliged to fit their plan inside changing the ground rules laid down for non-military considerations, which often had serious operational disadvantages.[10]

---

8. U.S. Department of State, "Memorandum No. 1 From the Cuban Study Group to President Kennedy," in *Foreign Relations of the United States, 1961-1963,* Volume X, *Cuba 1961-1962* (Washington: U.S. Government Printing Office, 1997), 576-600.

9. U.S. Department of State, "Memorandum No. 3 From the Cuban Study Group to President Kennedy," in *Foreign Relations of the United States, 1961-1963,* Volume X, *Cuba 1961-1962* (Washington: U.S. Government Printing Office, 1997), 603 (item a).

10. Ibid. (item b).

4. Another aspect pointed out in the report refers to the presentation of content and significance of the operation to political leaders. In the report it is thus expressed that: "The leaders of the operation did not always present their case with sufficient force and clarity to the senior officials of the Government to allow the latter to appreciate the consequences of some of their decisions. This remark applies in particular to the circumstances surrounding the cancellation of the D-day strikes."[11]

5. It is clearly specified that perspectives of success were doubtful from the lack of integrality in the focus with which the operation mounted, because according to the report:

There was a marginal character of the operation which increased with each additional limitation and cast a serious doubt over its ultimate success. The landing force was small in relation to its 36-mile beachhead and to the probable enemy reaction. The air support was short of pilots if the beach was to require cover for a long period. There were no fighters to keep off such Castro airplanes as might escape the initial air strikes. . . .[12]

6. It is evident that groups of information and analysis of the CIA involved in the operation were incapable of undertaking accurate diagnosis and prospects in relation to the measures of response that Cuba would unleash before the landing. They did not recognize the truth of the operational situation undertaken in a country in revolution; they fell in the trap of the ideology that justified their plans and did not put into practice scientific principles, based on political, sociological, psychological, and military studies. In terms of Marxist science it can be stated that there was no relation between the objective and subjective factor. Thus, what apparently is a philosophical problem turned into a political disaster.

7. President Kennedy was not appropriately informed on alternatives that would be present in case the Assault Brigade failed to sustain the beachhead. He approved the operation thinking that in case the Brigade did not keep control of such a place, guerilla warfare would then be put into practice.

8. Installation of the senior offices in charge of directing operations from a general headquarters in Washington made perception of what was happening in the theater of operations difficult; it also provoked that

11. Ibid. (item c).
12. Ibid. (item d).

chiefs of the expeditionary group did not have opportune access to required information to operate.

9. There was no clear or explicit position, rather determining, concerning the feasibility of the operation on the part of the DOD in which different factors intervened. Thus, the report expresses that:

... By acquiescing in the Zapata Plan, they gave the impression to others of approving it although they had expressed their preference for Trinidad at the outset, a point which apparently never reached the senior civilian officials. As a body they reviewed the successive changes of the plan piecemeal and only within a limited context, a procedure which was inadequate procedure for the proper examination of all military ramifications. Individually, they had differing understandings of important features of the operation apparently arising from oral briefings in absence of written documents.[13]

10. From the study undertaken, it was evident that the NSC had wrongly directed the operation in such a way that the intelligence community, the institutions represented at the NSC, the President's advisors and the executive itself failed to undertake and design a correct strategy. Therefore, this was not a simple defeat of the CIA plans, but of a whole policy that would have required other means, methods and forms to face a revolution backed up by a whole people willing to continue forwards in the political, social, and economic changes despite the proposals of the United States. Kennedy had no other choice but to personally assume the political cost of the failure, even though he would not renounce to destroy the revolutionary work. New pledges would be undertaken, and new threats of aggression would hang over Cuba.

It was necessary, therefore, to establish new courses of action, because as the report concludes:

... in the light of the foregoing considerations, we are of the opinion that the preparation and execution of paramilitary operations such as Zapata are a form of Cold War action in which the country must be prepared to engage. If it does so, it must engage in it with a maximum chance of success. Such operations should be planned and executed by a governmental mechanism capable of bringing

13. Ibid., (item h).

into play, in addition to military and covert techniques, all other forces, political, ideological, economic and intelligence, which can contribute to its success. No such mechanism presently exists, but should be created to plan, coordinate and further a national Cold War strategy capable of including paramilitary operations.[14]

In the minds of the authors of the report submitted to the President to determine the causes and conditions of failure of the operation and new directions to promote against Cuba was already present the Operation Mongoose.

In the late '90s two important documents on the CIA failure at the Bay of Pigs were released: the General Inspector Lyman Kirkpatrick's report and the assessment of Col. Jack Hawkins' main military planner of the Operation Pluto. Both documents contribute to the analysis of causes and conditions that explain the U.S. assessment on the failure of the operation, provide considerations, assessments and judgments concerning the mistakes committed by the CIA, from the tactical and strategic viewpoint.

In July 1961, a plan of the United States Central Intelligence Agency was known, whose proposals were pointing to deepen subversive actions on Cuba.[15] This plan pointed to the creation of a broad organization of resistance to be subject to the CIA control. That is, agents and internal resources under a control and direction of the CIA; to support counter-revolutionary organizations inland that were willing to generate clandestine operations; and to create bases of primary operations in the United States. In this way, the CIA aspired to create a clandestine movement in the Island sustained in its operational interests, instead of a clandestine movement sustained in the criterion to build an independent counterrevolutionary political force to face the Revolution.

Absence of identification in relation to the tactics to follow between Kennedy and the CIA's advisors would be a constant that will always be present during the whole Kennedy's presidential period. In fact, both Kennedy and his advisors recognized, after the Bay of Pigs, the political need to rebuild the Central Intelligence Agency to empower it in order to face challenges of new times.

---

14. Ibid., 605 (item 2).
15. Released document of the Main Assistant of the United States President (Schlesinger) to the Associate Main Advisor of the President (Richard Goodwin). Cuban State Security Historical Research Center (CIHSE) Archives.

In the second half of July 1961, President Kennedy examined the pros and the cons of an intervention in Cuba. In that sense, he consults Admiral Arleigh Burke if indeed the United States would have to intervene in Cuba. Burke's response did not wait: the United States necessarily would have to intervene, then Kennedy asked Admiral Burke if the Island could easily be occupied, to which he responded that every time this was getting more difficult. Then, Kennedy asked another question: What would happen if the United States intervenes in Cuba? Burke answered that this would be a hell, but someday the United States would have to do it.

In a very interesting way it is observed that on August 16, 1961, during a meeting of the Joint Chief of Staff (JCS) of the Armed Forces of the United States, a contingency plan in case of violence against the Naval Base at Guantánamo was examined. Coincidentally, and not for mere chance, in this period plots to assassinate Commander in Chief had the involvement of the U.S. Navy placed at the Base.

The referred contingency plan, elaborated from a supposed Cuban provocation against the Naval Base at Guantánamo to cause the beginning of hostilities, present the following aspects:
- Defense of the Naval Base at Guantánamo;
- Contributing to establish a friendly government to the United States interest;
- Restoring and keeping the order.

The measures of the plan contemplate the blockade to Cuba, reinforcement in the Base and amphibious air attack on the Island.

On August 22, 1961, President Kennedy's advisor, Richard Goodwin, made an assessment in relation to the Organization of American States (OAS) Conference held in Punta del Este, called by the United States to propose concrete actions on Cuba. The Cuban delegation that attended the conference was headed by Commander Ernesto "Che" Guevara, who during his participation, made public the stance of the Cuban Revolution in matters of foreign policy.

When assessing the results of the conference, Goodwin pointed out that any hope of action of the OAS on Cuba was condemned to failure, because big countries like Mexico and Brazil opposed to such action.

Richard Goodwin, one of the main architects of the Kennedy administration policy towards Cuba formulated recommendations in relation to actions to be developed:

19

1. Paying low public attention to the Cuban problem to prevent Cuba from being considered a "victim of the United States policy;"

2. Intensifying moderately, measures of economic pressure on Cuba, as well as undertaking sabotage in key sectors of the economy and implementing in all its dimension the Act of Trade with the Enemy of the United States Treasure Department;

3. Developing moderately military pressure, such as not divulged sea maneuvers near the Cuban coastline, reinforcing the Naval Base at Guantánamo, and spreading false information;

4. Continuing and increasing covert operations aimed at first of all destroying economic centers and delivering resources for activities to be undertaken by members of counterrevolutionary organizations, with political and ideological objectives;

5. Increasing propaganda work pointing to: account the Cuban people how their government is sacrificing their welfare in favor of international communism; broadly divulge economic failures of the Cuban Government in Latin America and the Caribbean; create the Security Pact of the Caribbean as a strictly defensive measure;

6. Beginning the study of possible conflicts that might exist in the top Cuban leadership.

ACTIVITIES OF THE CENTRAL INTELLIGENCE AGENCY AND COUNTERREVOLUTIONARY ORGANIZATIONS IN THE COUNTRY, IN THE PERIOD POST-BAY OF PIGS TO LATE 1961. THE POLITICAL ARENA

From the defeat of the Assault Brigade 2506, still with the taste of powder in the battlefield, the Central Intelligence Agency compelled in unleashing flash operations aimed at destroying, by means of armed violence in the most immediate time, the Cuban Revolution. An important study of this period is found in Fabián Escalante Font book, *La Guerra Secreta de la CIA contra Cuba* [The CIA Secret War on Cuba], where principal aims, directions of work and intentions that characterized the CIA and the counterrevolutionary activity in the period April-November 1961 are examined.

A whole of factors intervene and are related among them to explain the high aggressiveness degree showed by the CIA and the U.S. Government:

1. The defeat of the Assault Brigade 2506 was the hardest setback experienced by John F. Kennedy in his political life.

The failure of the Bay of Pigs exposed him to a strong criticism not only from the ranks of Republicans, but even in the own Democratic ranks. A crisis of credibility in the executive to lead the destinies of the nation emerged. Kennedy felt compelled to return the strike at any cost.

2. Bay of Pigs also meant the strongest setback of the Central Intelligence Agency since its creation in 1947. Langley's mystical theology, Allen Dulles's legend and the myth of invincibility of the United States vanished in only seventy-two hours in April 1961.

The Central Intelligence Agency and its director Allen Dulles knew that they had to go for the search of the lost time in the Operation Pluto and hit a deadly and final strike to the Cuban Revolution in the coming months. Otherwise, Kennedy would decide what he had already reflected on: to restructure and rebuild the CIA with other cadres, particularly those who did not intervene in the Operation Pluto. For the CIA. destroying the Revolution meant the physical elimination of Commander in Chief Fidel Castro and other leaders of the Revolution. This event would associate with an armed uprising in search of assistance of the United States and the OAS, a coverage under which the direct military intervention of the U.S. troops would camouflage.

3. The counterrevolutionary organizations were going through a critical phase of their existence from the dismantling of the Revolutionary United Front (FUR) leadership, in March 1961, which had eliminated the perspectives of an armed uprising coinciding with the landing of the Assault Brigade 2506. Had the FUR achieved its objectives of unity in the country, the principal counterrevolutionary organizations operating in Cuba would be present. The recovery of the counterrevolution would depend on high degree from the logistic support of the CIA, as well as the assembling of new structures of the counterrevolution that operated in the Island.

Between June and December 1961 the Cuban authorities discovered and frustrated important plots to assassinate Fidel Castro Ruz. One of these plans was aimed at promoting instability in the country and to unleash the U.S. military intervention. The United States Central Intelligence Agency and the Naval Intelligence Service of the Naval Base at Guantánamo organized the Operation Patty as it was called by the foe.

The principal objective was to assassinate Fidel and Raúl during the celebration of acts for July 26 in La Habana and Oriente provinces.

The plan related with the undertaking of self-provocation in the Base, sabotage and uprisings in order to create conditions for the military intervention of the U.S. troops. Alfredo Izaguirre de la Riva and other U.S. intelligence agents, who had been infiltrated into the country, were under arrest.[16]

In October, the Cuban authorities frustrated the so-called Operation Liborio, complex subversive program mounted by the CIA through the counterrevolutionary organization Revolutionary Movement of the People (MRP). In that project, the assassination of Fidel Castro and other leaders of the Revolution was conceived during a rally to be held on October 4, 1961, in front of the northern terrace of the former Presidential Palace. The idea was to shoot a bazooka to the tribune from a neighboring building and to throw grenades to the crowd. Reynold González, coordinator of the MRP, Dalia Jorge, Manuel Izquierdo, underchief of the MRP and others were arrested.[17] Terrorist actions, sabotage to economic centers and operations of psywar were projected in the Operation Liborio. Of these, the most important one was Operation Peter Pan, a Machiavellian project of the State Department, the CIA, and the U.S. Catholic Church. Through misinformation and black propaganda, they provoked legal trips of about 14,000 children who traveled to the United States without parents custody to prevent the supposed expatriation to the USSR to be dictated by an Act on parents custody, faked by CIA agents.[18]

The plans of assassination above mentioned, as well as the Operation Peter Pan, were actions of State terrorism legally proved and documented. Proofs on the CIA involvement were frequent, and its connection with counterrevolutionary organizations. The operations Patty and Liborio were structured after the creation of the Executive Action Group. This was a body designed by the CIA to plan and execute programmed assassinations against heads of State hostile to the U.S. policy (as in the case of Patrice Lumumba), or not convenient for the continuity

16. Ministry of the Interior (MININT), "Candela" [Fire] Case Record, 1961. CIHSE Archives.
17. Raúl Roldán, Major of the MININT, interviewed by the author, regarding the "Terraza Norte" [Northern Terrace] Case, 1998. CIHSE Archives.
18. Ministry of the Interior (MININT), "Imprenta" [Printing] and "Peter Pan" Cases Records, 1961. CIHSE Archives.

of a determined policy (Trujillo). Would it be a mere chance that the chief of the Executive Action, William Harvey, was also in charge of the Cuban Task Force (a CIA Operational Group) after the Bay of Pigs? And how to explain, according to the human rights, the adulteration of a parents custody Act that instigated children's migration to the United States?

After the Bay of Pigs, the CIA could not create counterrevolutionary structures capable of setting the foundation of an inner movement opposed to the Revolution, neither was it capable of establishing a strong cohesive impenetrable intelligence system.

The CIA failures and the counterrevolution in the period after the Bay of Pigs until the authorization of the Operation Mongoose in November 1961 need to be completely examined and, therefore, to determine their causes and conditions.

A fundamental mistake in the work of the U.S. intelligence resides in not having undertaken an objective, opportune and current survey of the existing operational situation in the Cuban arena after the Bay of Pigs; it proves the lack of truly intelligence estimates. Had the operational situation been analyzed correctly, the CIA would have had to redesign its tactics and strategies with other means, methods and working objectives. The focuses supported by voluntarism and empiricism oriented its actions, compelled by the frenzy of Kennedy administration from the defeat of the Brigade 2506.

The enemy was incapable of modeling the confrontation system that the State Security used, and exposed its agents to opportune and accurate penetration of our agents. The organization structures created by the counterrevolution inland were transgressed by operational measures of confrontation; that is, the State Security knew the foe, the foe did not know the *modus operandi* of the Security, probably it was underestimated. Imperial arrogance prevented men of Langley to imagine that Cuban agents might misinform and skillfully manipulate its officials trained in the most convulsive regions of the world. In the operational work, a form of class struggle is expressed: revolutionary agents and officials *versus* counterrevolutionary agents and officials. In our case it was, in its highest expression, the secret confrontation fought between the people and imperialism.

The CIA calculations concerning the potential of opposition were unfortunate. They supposed that most people did not back up the Revolution, or were indifferent to it; they could have developed social-and-operational studies with secret and public information, and the evidence would have proved a broadly majority back up to the Revolution.

The CIA claim to create political and social conditions to allow unleashing inner uprising and, therefore, to provoke the direct military intervention of the United States, with or without OAS coverage, supported itself on false premises. What political forces of the Cuban society was the CIA supporting on for such actions? The Cuban bourgeoisie (its fundamental elements) had migrated to the Mecca of capitalism; its economic power was destroyed by nationalization of August and October 1960 turning into socialist the Cuban economy before the proclamation of the socialist character of the Revolution's ideology and policy in April 1961, in the middle of the deployment of Operation Pluto (April 16, 1961). The first Agrarian Reform of May 1959 had broken the power of Cuban landowners and of the big U.S. consortia, which had invested their capital in Cuban land. The Cuban middle class or the small bourgeoisie assumed divergent positions: a part completely identified itself with the Revolution, another part kept apart indifferent, while another part confronted, in alliance to the bourgeoisie, and actively participated in the first counterrevolutionary organizations, of a very strong terrorist character. The working class, remembering Karl Marx, had reencoun-tered in the Revolution and fully participated in the revolutionary process as the most complete expression of the socialist project. Meanwhile, peasantry, almost all, fully participated in pro of a process that had eliminated the different kinds of exploitation to which they were subdued in the capitalist agrarian economy of the Cuban neocolonial republic.

Most Cuban intellectuality, had joined with their talent and creativeness the revolutionary process. Poets, writers, and artists not only created the National Union of Cuban Writers and Artists (UNEAC), but also they joined the Revolutionary National Militia, after the university students created the University Militia.

In the early years of the Revolution a close and organic connection between the position assumed by the highest catholic clergy and the development of counterrevolutionary organizations, such as Montecristi, MRP, MRR, DRE and others were to be established. Many of their leaders had been in the catholic youth and student movement.

Untimely plans of the CIA and its counterrevolutionary branches inland and abroad, designed in the period between April to late 1961, were destroyed by the strategy that the Revolution designed for their confrontation. The enemy did not spare human resources, technical means, or money to subvert the Revolution. The enemy simply did not recognize the capability of a people, a nation, to resist, to fight, and to overcome.

In the late 1961 new and gloomy plans and aggressions were conceived by the U.S. Government on Cuba; counterrevolutionary violence was merging from Florida coast against the Key of the Gulf, with the most secret and evil operation ever mounted by the United States intelligence community: the Operation Mongoose.

CHAPTER II. The Operation Mongoose: Myths and Realities

BACKGROUNDS

On June 18, 1948, the U.S. NSC issued the Directive NSC 10/2 authorizing the creation of an organization of covert actions, with the name of Office for Political Coordination (OPC). The directive established as the only limitation that these actions were developed in such a way that the United States Government involvement was not evident to non-authorized individuals, and in case that these actions were found out, the U.S. Government was ready to plausibly refuse any responsibility in these actions. The Directive NSC 10/2 defined the covert operations as an activity referred to propaganda, economic warfare, direct preventive action, including sabotage, anti-sabotage, measures of demolition and evacuation, subversion against hostile states, including assistance to clandestine groups and support to anti-Communist national elements in countries of the Free World threatened.[1]

This conception was to be the core of the subversive doctrine that the U.S. Government fostered against Cuba prior the Bay of Pigs, in the Operation Pluto and subsequently during Operation Mongoose.

On June 4, 1961, and at proposal of the Military Advisor of President John F. Kennedy, Gen. Maxwell Taylor, the Counter-Insurgency

---

1. These aspects are considered in Thomas Powers, *The Man Who Kept the Secrets. Richard Helms and the CIA* (New York: Alfred A. Knopf, 1979).

Group was created to face, through covert operations, the world revolutionary movement. This group was made up by:
- McGeorge Bundy, representative of the White House;
- Robert Kennedy, Attorney General;
- Allen Dulles, CIA. Subsequently, in September 1961, with Dulles's substitution as director of the CIA, John McCone would take his place;
- Gen. Lyman Lemnitzer, Chief of the Joint Chief of Staff;
- Roswell Gilpatrick, Deputy Secretary of Defense;
- Edward Murrow, of the U.S. Information Agency;
- Alexis Johnson, second Under-Secretary of State for Political Affairs.

As it was agreed, Cuba would be the first working line for the Counter-Insurgency Group. Subsequently, a second committee, the Special Group Augmented (SGA) was created to supervise anti-Cuban operations.

On November 1, 1961, President's Assistant Special Counsel (Richard Goodwin), issued an analysis report addressed to Kennedy, in which he made proposals establishing the guidelines for the new subversive policy on Cuba. The presidential advisor's thesis was based on the following considerations:
- The "command operation" is the only effective way to handle an all-out attack on the so-called Cuban problem, aimed at the downfall of the Revolution, or, at least, to reinforce underground, better propaganda, and access to more accurate and objective intelligence;
- Direction of this operation is conceived in a structure outside the State Department, due to the character of covert activities to undertake, but it is recommended that CIA not to be the leading force, because this has to reorganize its operations and thinking;
- Robert Kennedy is proposed as the most effective commander of this operation.[2]

These proposals have to be considered from the historic context where they were formulated. It is evident that CIA was going through a crisis of confidence concerning its operational capability to generate intelligence estimates, which reflected the Cuban operational situation. Likewise, CIA was considered to be the maximum responsible for not

2. U.S. Department of State, "Memorandum From the President's Assistant Special Counsel (Goodwin) to President Kennedy," in *Foreign Relations of the United States, 1961-1963,* Volume X, *Cuba 1961-1962* (Washington: U.S. Printing Office, 1997), 664-665.

having forged effective counterrevolutionary structures in the country; it was thought that CIA was not in conditions to establish a new strategy on the manner to face the Revolution.

Robert Kennedy's proposal to command this operation meant that the president would have a man of absolute confidence and of broad acceptance among the closest collaborators of John F. Kennedy. In practice, Robert Kennedy would be the second chief of the Operation Mongoose. John F. Kennedy had also thought in appointing Robert as new Director of the CIA when Dulles was replaced in September 1961, but refrained from making the proposal for fear to be pointed out in concentrating too much power in the Executive. John McCone would be the Director of the CIA.

An aspect to have into consideration, also, is that Cuba was completely perceived in the context of the Cold War, which characterizes this period, of the East-West conflict. At the same time, this is interpreted as an objective of the counter-insurgency program, drawn by the Kennedy administration, against movements of national liberation worldwide. For the rest, Cuba was framed from the perspective of threat to the United States national security and hemisphere security of the Latin American area, sphere of vital influence for the United States. In short, subversion and terrorism have been part, from the U.S. view, of the historic conflict between both nations.

THE OPERATION MONGOOSE SHOWS UP ON THE SCENE

By late November, the U.S. NSC issued a document addressed to the secretaries of State and Defense, the Attorney General, Gen. Maxwell Taylor, Gen. Landsdale, and Richard Goodwin. In the document, the United Sates President's decisions concerning the Operation Cuba, which would be later called Mongoose, are expressed. These decisions were adopted from proposals elaborated by Gen. Landsdale, which were to be outlined in January 1962. The recommendations formulated by the President's Assistant Special Counsel (Richard Goodwin) were considered in those decisions.

In the directions drawn by the National Security Council for the Operation Cuba, the use of all the resources available for the downfall of the Revolution was proposed. The president appointed Gen. Landsdale Chief of Operations of Cuba Program, which was to be directed through appropriate organizations and governmental departments. The group 5412 of the NSC must be informed in details of the activities in order to give advisory and formulate recommendations. This group, formed in 1955 by means of two directives of the NSC, was in charge of the final approval of all covert operations that CIA considered big, important, or sensitive as for obtaining presidential approval.

The secretaries of State and Defense were responsible, together with the Director of the CIA, to appoint senior officials to help the Chief of Operations in fulfilling the assigned missions. These officials exerted operational control on aspects of the operations related with Cuba, executed by departments that they represented.

The Operation Cuba was classified as top secret. Only the secretaries of State and Defense, the Attorney General, the Chief of Operations and the members of the Group 5412 could have access to it. Some of its plans would be part of the so-called "jewels of the CIA": the most secret, the deepest, the most compartmentalized operations and which violated, de facto, the limits established for covert operations. Plots to assassinate heads of State and even plans of doing medical experiments in human beings were among these "jewels."[3]

In December 1961, the new CIA Director, John McCone, replaced Richard Bisell in his responsibilities for operations on Cuba and this was assigned to Richard Helms, Deputy Director for Operations, mainly due to John F. Kennedy pressures, who was discontent for the failures of the CIA operations after the Bay of Pigs. Cuba became an independent operational section within the Western Hemisphere Department of the Central Intelligence Agency.

In the late 1961 or early 1962, William K. Harvey was appointed Chief of Task Force W, the CIA unit within the Operation Mongoose. According to the investigator Thomas Powers,

. . . from that moment [he refers to late 1961] the CIA initiated a serious effort under close supervision of the White House. But in this occasion, the operation was undertaken as an authentic clandestine operation, cautiously secret, and from the point of view of all, but Cuba, quietly. Castro was not overthrown, but neither confronted Kennedy difficulties for his pledge and failure; the security was so steady that the so-called Operation Mongoose was unknown

---

3. William Colby mentioned the main "jewels of the CIA" in William Colby and Peter Forbath, *Honorable Man* (New York: Simon & Schuster, 1978).

for over ten years. In the long run, things were not better for Helms than what had been for Bisell, but kept the operation away from papers.[4]

Some authors argue that the story of the name of this operation, Mongoose, is more or less like that: Landsdale asked a CIA official of the Cuba Bureau to seek a coded-name for the group working with Cuba in the Department of Defense. The official asked the Cipher Department for old-fashion ciphers of the Far East, thinking that he could hide that Cuba would be Mongoose objective. The two first letters of the cipher indicate the geographical area. The letters *MO* referred to Thailand. The CIA official chose the word *Mongoose* of the inactive ciphers and gave it to Landsdale. *Mongoose* was never used at the CIA. The coded-name for Cuba at the CIA was *Am*.

In the chronology edited in 1996 by National Security Archive, on the occasion of a debate at a scholar conference on the events concerning the failure of the Bay of Pigs and actions undertaken by the U.S. Government subsequently, it is stated:

> November 4, 1961. A major new covert action program aimed at overthrowing Cuban government was developed during a meeting at the White House. The new program code named Operation Mongoose was to be run by counter-insurgency specialist Edward G. Landsdale. A high-level inter-agency group, the Special Group Augmented (SGA), was created with the sole purpose of overseeing Operation Mongoose. A memorandum formally establishing Mongoose was signed by President Kennedy on November 30.[5]

All operations and actions of Mongoose that were to be generated on Cuba are established in a paper presented by Gen. Landsdale to President Kennedy on January 18, 1962, under the name of Cuba Project. Its main objective was to establish that the United States assisted the Cuban counterrevolution to overthrow the Cuban Revolution from within and establish a new government, friendly to the United States.

---

4. Thomas Powers, *The Man Who Kept the Secrets: Richard Helms and the CIA* (New York: Alfred A. Knopf, 1979).

5. "Chronology," in National Security Archives, *The Cuban Missile Crisis, 1962*, Volume 1, Project Editor Laurence Chang (Alexandria: Chadwyck-Healy, Inc., 1990).

The requirements to provoke an internal uprising against the Revolution contemplated various aspects: the convenience of a movement of political actions, strongly motivated and established within Cuba, combined with economic warfare aimed at provoking the failure of the Revolution in its eagerness for solving economic needs, and to unleash psychological operations. Together, it is planned the creation of groups of military character in charge of sabotage and terrorism actions according to political objectives.

When conceiving this project, the U.S. experts in counter-insurgency could not fail to recognize that the failure of the Assault Brigade 2506 psychologically unbalanced the counterrevolution and provoked a loss of trust about the capability and intentions of the United States Government in order to destroy the Revolution.

Actions of Mongoose required the support of other nations of the continent, and the propaganda on Cuba was to be founded in the supposed foreign-condition character of the Revolution and the political imperative to defend the Western Hemisphere from communism.

The preparatory phase of Mongoose had the objective to organize political actions within Cuba with their own means for internal communications, psychological operations and its own group of actions (small guerrilla groups, sabotage groups, etc.).

As *conditione sine qua non* it was the euphoric back up of most Cuban people and to let known this to all over the world. According to CIA experts in counter-insurgency most Cuban people did not back up the Revolution, while apathy and indifference prevailed in the operational theater. Similar assessments prove a high degree of misinformation and lack of knowledge of what was happening in Cuba in 1961 and 1962. The people reaction before the aggression of the Assault Brigade 2506 had reiterated an unquestionable reality: more than 90% of the Cuban people actively defended their revolution. The counterrevolution lacked of a social basis to foster its actions, and the existence of its organization structures completely depended on the CIA support. At the same time, this indicated the lack of capability and the impossibility of the counterrevolutionary organizations to elaborate its own working directions. Thus, it had to do what the CIA ordered to be done, independently of the feasibility and objectivity. The principles of political and operational rationality were not present in the guidelines of the CIA work.

In the deployment of actions of Mongoose, the so-called "climatic moment" is mentioned, which should be the source of all actions included in the operation. According them, the climatic moment of the revolt would take place from a reaction of discontent of the people before a governmental action unleashed by an incident, or by the break-ing of leading cadres within the regime, or both. A main objective of the project was to foster such a situation.

The chain of actions is assessed in this way: climatic moment - open rebellion - occupation of zones - request of assistance to other countries of the Western Hemisphere. According to other nations of the Western Hemisphere, the United States would offer military support to the re-bellion.

The institutions represented in the operational team of Mongoose were: Department of State, Central Intelligence Agency, Deparment of Defense, and the United States Information Agency.

As it was indicated in the assessments submitted by Landsdale in the context of the Cuban Project, the CIA undertook a special poll to interrogate Cuban refugees in the United States. Between 1700 and 2000 Cubans were arriving in the United Sates every month. The CIA intelli-gence resources in the Island were limited, therefore it was required to increase intelligence there in quantity and depth.

An interesting recommendation of Landsdale was that the elabora-tion of political platform of the counterrevolutionary organizations that would operate in Cuba in the context of Mongoose was the responsibil-ity of the institutions (Department of State and CIA) of the United States Government. This political platform was based on the need to create popular support for the internal uprising.

It was recognized the CIA lack of capability to guarantee agents of political action to support the purposes of the internal uprising; and they proposed the selection of eight to ten Cuban agents of political action for February. They would be chosen among the emigreés.

It was the CIA job to locate twenty zones in the Island in order to establish the groups of action for February 1, 1962. Priority is given to La Habana and localities in Las Villas.

The diplomatic actions contemplated in the Cuban Project comprised actions of the Department of State concerning the meeting of the OAS Foreign Ministers to accomplish a broad consensus in the Western Hemi-sphere about the policy to be followed with Cuba, condemn it diplomati-cally and isolate it from the Hemisphere. It is also considered the use of diplomatic actions in order to stimulate the internal revolt in Cuba. Like-wise, the need to implement economic actions aimed at blockading Cuba's trade is argued. It is very interesting, from the operational viewpoint, the sabotage plan of the sugar harvest.

The Department of Defense was the responsible for the prepara-tion of a military contingency plan—military intervention of the United

States—in the event the counterrevolution requested assistance when the popular uprising broke out.

The analysis elaborated around the operational situation in Cuba is not favorable for the plans of the Department of State and the Central Intelligence Agency, according to the following:

Both State and CIA are continuing to explore their capabilities (with results largely negative to date) for mounting special group operations inside Cuba focused upon dynamic elements of the population, particularly through the Church to reach women and families and through Labor contacts to reach workers. Other elements include enlistment of the youth and professional groupings. Special consideration is to be given to doing this through Latin American operational contacts.[6]

According to Landsdale, what was expressed in his text was vital for the success of the political action when the CIA achieve the fulfillment of these objectives.

Assesments expressed concerning the almost null feasibility for the deployment of operations of the agents of political action are not wrong. In this analysis the big drama of the CIA and the counterrevolution encircles: How is it possible to subvert the order in an unsubvertible society like the Cuban one? What mechanism can the CIA and the counterrevolution use to seek points of counterrevolutionary support? What forms and structures can they be sustained in? Without objective conditions, or appropriate subjective factors (there was absence of social classes that might be counterrevolutionary performers. Also the counterrevolution lacked a native and autonomous ideology, it was essentially Plattist, neo-annexionist and organically dependent of the United States policy), what other choice did Mongoose have, other than exporting counterrevolution to Cuba, exporting subversive action, intelligence activity, terrorism, attempts to crime, operations of political-and-ideological diversion? Who, but the United States Government with its funds would cover the expenses of this operation?

When analyzing its potentialities for mounting clandestine operations in Cuba, the CIA experts considered conclusively that the image of

6. U.S. Department of State, "Program Review by the Chief of Operations, Operation Mongoose (Landsdale)," in *Foreign Relations of the United States, 1961-1963,* Volume X, *Cuba 1961-1962* (Washington: U.S. Printing Office, 1997), 714 (item k).

a supposed movement of popular opposition in Cuba should be created in order to achieve support from outside, to improve the CIA operational capability, and to provoke a climate to allow actions of support to overt operations.

The directions, purposes and objectives (DPO) of Mongoose comprised thirty-two tasks corresponding to intelligence (four), political (six), economic (thirteen), psychological (four), and military action (five) areas.

Intelligence tasks proposed the recollection of information concerning internal situation in Cuba through interviews with refugees in Florida and other states of the United States; reanalysis of capability of agents in Cuba, as well as information gathering recruiting sources in third countries.

Concerning tasks of political character, they proposed the elaboration of desertion plans of revolutionary leaders in the high level aimed at breaking the moral and ideology of the Revolution; the design of covert, diversionist, and misinformation actions constituted a priority level for the CIA, in order to undermine stability of the Cuban Government; the elaboration of a program for the popular uprising in Cuba, which demanded chosen actions within Cuba, evaluation of recruited agents, their infiltration, assignment of tasks, as well as presentation of the political platform of the opposition. Besides, it was important to know the operational situation of the counterrevolutionary organizations inland and their insertion in the plans of the CIA. On the one hand, an important place of political tasks referred to the activity that the United States should undertake through the OAS to obtain solidarity of their governments with the actions of the counterrevolution. On the other hand, the Department of State would create an operational mechanism in the Caribbean area to undertake actions on Cuba with the complicity of local governments. The political tasks included the selection of population groups in Cuba where the United States intelligence services could dynamically work on.

The economic warfare on the Cuban nation acquired a priorized dimension in the United States subversion strategy. In that sense, the reinforcement of blockade measures and seeking the involvement of Latin American states in this enterprise was conceived. Such measures comprised actions referred to Cuban trade in the Latin American area; implementation of special licenses for exports to Cuba from Latin American countries; export controls for Cuba, similar to the ones established for trade with China and the USSR; prohibition to U.S. ships from direct or indirect involvement in trade with Cuba; prohibition of using the U.S. seaports; studies on the feasibility to prevent access to U.S. seaports of Soviet and Eastern-Europe ships, which are involved in busines with Cuba; drawing policies for not to authorize that subsidiaries of U.S. enterprises negotiate with Cuba, as well as requesting the cooperation of the National Council of Foreign Trade, the Chamber of Commerce, and the National Association of the United States Manufacturers in the development of the blockade on Cuba.

In the psychological tasks, campaigns of propaganda pointing to distort Cuba's state of affairs abroad were present, while the counterrevolution in Cuba was presented as a David against Goliath, facing the communist domination and they aspired to mobilize world solidarity with these actions. Another side of the campaigns sought to reflect the retaliation measures that would be adopted against leaders and sectors of the population, once the Revolution was defeated. Thus, these must be accused in the counterrevolutionary Cuba as criminals of the people. The CIA and the USIA would create symbols, songs, and themes of propaganda for the counterrevolution, while searching ways to introduce smuggled packages with food and counterrevolutionary mottoes.

The work for planning military actions covered the elaboration of a plan of military contingency that established the military intervention in Cuba of the United States Armed Forces in support of the counterrevolutionary movement; plans to develop sabotage in the Island; studies on the involvement of Cubans enlisted in the U.S. Army, in actions in Cuba, in order to develop special operations.

The thirty-two tasks of Mongoose should be planned and submitted in February 1962. Plans had to be immediately elaborated.

In a meeting held with representatives of the Pentagon and the Central Intelligence Agency, the Attorney General, Robert Kennedy, on behalf of the president told the following views:

(e) Accordingly, a solution to the Cuban problem today carries "The top priority in the United States Government—all else is secondary—no time, money, effort, or manpower is to be spared. There can be no misunderstandings on the involvement of the agencies concerned, nor on the responsibility to carry out this job. The agency heads understand that you are to have a full backing on what you need."

35

(f) . . . the President indicated . . . "the final chapter on Cuba has not been written"—it's got to be done and will be done.[7]

In February, the Chief of Operation Mongoose made a balance on the situation in Cuba, from which the actions to undertake would be developed. In these approaches ideologizing criteria, such as, "the Communist regime is an active Sino-Soviet Bloc spearhead in our Hemisphere and that Communist controls inside Cuba are severe. . . . an anti-regime atmosphere has been created among Cuban people,"[8] are observed. And in the analyses undertaken he concluded that time is against subversive plans designed in Mongoose. He also stressed that the thirty-two tasks of the project were the basis of subversive work on Cuba, and he concluded, "The course of action set forth herein is realistic within present operation estimates and intelligence. . . . It aims for a revolt which can take place in Cuba by October 1962."[9]

Also in February, in a new document of the Cuba Project (February 20, 1962), the Plan of Basic Action within Cuba was made known, in which actions and purposes to develop were established.

Infiltration of three agents in the country to explore areas chosen by the CIA in order to study operational conditions and working requirements was planned in March.

According to released documents, between April and June 1962, various actions were planned. Infiltration up to five additional agents in areas chosen by the CIA was foreseen in April, in order to report on the counterrevolutionary potential and to begin new radio transmission against Cuba, whose essential objective was to sow the idea that indeed a clandestine movement was operating in Cuba.

The undertaking of new operation of agents and delivery of supplies for enemy activity was determined for May. Infiltration of twelve additional agents, in June, in areas previously chosen by the CIA was planned, as well as the creation of three clandestine networks under the order of

---

7. U.S. Department of State, "Memorandum from the Chief of Operations in the Deputy Directorate from Plans (Helms) to Director of Central Intelligence McCone," in *Foreign Relations of the United States, 1961-1963,* Volume X, *Cuba 1961-1962* (Washington: U.S. Printing Office, 1997), 720.

8. U.S. Department of State, "Program Review by the Chief of Operations,. Operation Mongoose (Landsdale)," in *Foreign Relations of the United States, 1961-1963,* Volume X, *Cuba 1961-1962* (Washington: U.S. Printing Office, 1997), 745.

9. Ibid., 746.

CIA infiltrated agents, and of bases for counterrevolutionary activities in the mountains. Also, a headquarters for counterrevolutionary leadership, with communications means to link with counterrevolutionary groups was conceived. Likewise, in order to obtain photographic and documentary evidence for information in campaigns of propaganda aimed at encouraging counterrevolutionary activities within Cuba, actions of psywar were planned.

The formation of five additional counterrevolutionary groups was proposed in July, as well as the organization of counterrevolutionary groups near airports and communications facilities, with the perspective to undertake sabotage actions, and the increase of infiltration spots and the undertaking of small sabotage.

For August, actions in factories and other places, at a snail's pace, were prepared as expression of passive resistance, actions of propaganda, formation of paramilitary groups and actions of groups in key areas in the mountains. The integration of the counterrevolutionary movement inland was planned, to increase the activity of terrorist groups in the mountains, the deployment of black propaganda by means of the elaboration and distribution of faked documents to the people, aimed at discrediting the Revolutionary Government; to provoke unfavorable moods in the people, and provoking conflicts inside and outside the governmental institutions. Also, the recruitment of counterrevolutionary combatants with volunteers of Latin America and other regions was programmed. Among the proposals, the creation of a so-called Battalion Martí, with foreign recruits from Latin America and camps of refugees from Eastern Europe was planned.

Significantly, actions against main leaders of the Revolution catalogued as "criminals of the people," and operations to release counterrevolutionary prisoners were planned.

In this same month, the blockade to any assistance from the Socialist Bloc to Cuba, through all means available for the counterrevolution inland, would take place: attacking ships with supplies from the Socialist Bloc, mining seaports, making sabotage to air transport, destroying goods in warehouses and undertaking actions against technicians of the Socialist Bloc working in Cuba. For September, sabotage against air-and-land transport and communications were established.

October was the key month for the final unchaining of unbalancing plans. This was the decisive effort of Mongoose to destroy the Revolution from inside with outside support. This was the historic challenge that once John F. Kennedy referred to. Final actions comprised the development of a general strike; the undertaking of demonstration against the Revolution; the pronouncement of the revolt and overt rebellion for the downfall of the Revolution.

In its instructions, the Operation Mongoose established:

When the popular movement is holding meaningful territory in Cuba it should form a provisional government. This should permit open Latin American and U.S. help, if requested and necessary. A military government situation will exist for the initial period and we must insist upon realism in this interim period preceding reasonable civilian control.[10]

The Plan of Basic Action, elegant literary term for the group of covert operations contemplated in the Operation Mongoose, was associated to a Plan of Political Support according to the objectives of the covert operations. This plan proposed the use of the OAS in order to condemn Communism in Cuba and to influence in world and Latin American public opinion. Officials of the United States Government and press sources at Washington level were to be instructed to offer political support. Also, in this plan, the engagement of the national prestige and the power of political, intellectual, labor, student, religious and military leaders were conceived for involvement in the cause of the Cuban people against the communist regime.

It was also stated the use of trade-union leaders of the counterrevolutionary emigration as well as of Latin American. The Cuban Revolutionary Council of José Miró Cardona would mobilize the groups of Cuban counterrevolutionaries living in the United States. Actions of propaganda were to be designed for Latin America in order to generate support for the counterrevolution in Cuba, and radio programs to provoke desideologizing processes in the Cuban society were to be made. Thus, religious programs, interviews with emigration workers belonging to the counterrevolution, students, fishermen, and families were to be developed, aimed at letting know the way of life to be retrieved in Cuba. It was pointed out that the CIA disposed special capabilities to broadcast to Cuba (Radio Swan) and to use transmission

10. Lawrence Chang, and Peter Kornbluh, ed., "Document 5: Brig. Gen. Edward Landsdale, 'The Cuba Project,' February 20, 1962, (program review and basic action plan for OPERATION MONGOOSE)," in *The Cuban Missile Crisis, 1962: A National Security Archive Documents Reader* (New York: New Press, 1992).

facilities in Miami, New Orleans, and in about seventy-five isles in the Caribbean zone.

In October, most Latin American countries would express the official political support to U.S. actions.

In developing Mongoose, a Plan of Economic Support, related to the Plan of Basic Action and the one of Political Support, was elaborated. Its methods proposed to accomplish the complete stagnation of the Cuban economy. Still, in U.S. documents an aspect, whose final objective was the annihilation of the Cuban economy, remained classified. The most important measures drawn in this plan consisted in deterring the OAS and allies to the United States to give up negotiating with Cuba. It was also contemplated to prevent access of U.S. merchandises to Cuba through third countries; the elaboration of lists of countries that would negotiate with Cuba; harassment to sea transport in trade relations with Cuba, and to dispose of assistance of U.S. enterprise groups to promote more active actions against Cuba. An important point referred to production of rumors to damage the sale of Cuban goods in other countries.

Operations of psywar accompanied all these plans. Actions of propaganda aimed at creating a "crusade for human liberty" were established; a center of transmission towards Cuba, to be presented as spokesman of the underground was designed. The U.S. politicians would visit the camps of Cuban refugees in Florida to express their solidarity. Publications of testimonies, elaborated by Cuban refugees in the United States were planned by assignment, and broad information coverage in the case of deserters was ordered.

The actions of military character were drawn in the Plan of Military Support. The first point consisted in offering logistic support in personnel and training to the actions of Mongoose. A established purpose referred to the intentions of undertaking actions against Cuba through military, bilateral, multilateral bodies, and, even, personal contacts with Latin American military men. At the same time, the increase of the U.S. military presence in the Caribbean was programmed; violations of air-and-sea space of Cuba; harassment of the Cuban civil aviation and ships; protection of counterrevolutionary groups when undertaking their actions against Cuba. It was also the responsibility of the Department of Defense the interference and the blockade of communications of Cuba.

In particular, a Plan of Support and Sabotage was elaborated. The objective was to disable important sectors of the Cuban economy, such as nickel, oil supply, destruction of the communication system of the country, and of electric plants in the western provinces.

The Plan of Support of Intelligence comprised various guidelines, according to the Plan of Basic Action of covert operations. In this sense, the full activation of the Office of Special Operations (JM-WAVE Station, principal center of the Operation Mongoose) and of the Office for Admission of Refugees at Opa Locka, Fla., was proposed, as well as the establishment of additional interrogation centers for émigrés. The increase of special intelligence, other sensitive intelligence coverage and the intelligence potential in the bosom of the counterrevolutionary emigration were important objectives. It was also conceived to develop the means of the inter-American Junta of Defense to offer substantial intelligence on activities of Cubans and periodical intelligence estimates.

SPECIAL OPERATIONS PROPOSALS OF THE DEPARTMENT OF DEFENSE (DOD)

On February 2, 1962, the representative of the DOD and of the Operations Group of the Caribbean, Gen. William H. Craig, submitted the Chief of Operations of Mongoose, Gen. Edward Landsdale, a group of ideas to be taken into consideration when elaborating the objectives of the Cuba Project (Operation Mongoose). These considerations were exposed, in general, in operations; each operation had a determined purpose. The assignment of operations was as follows:

1. Operation NO LOVE LOST
   Objective: To confuse and harass Castro Cuban Pilots by use of radio conversations.
2. Operation SMASHER
   Objective: The objective is to disrupt /disable military and commercial communications facilities in Cuba.
3. Operation FREE RIDE
   Objective: The objective is to create unrest and dissension amongst the Cuban people.
4. Operation TURN ABOUT
   Objective: The objective is to create indications to Fidel Castro that his value to the revolutionary cause has diminished to the point where plans are being made for his "removal."

5. Operation DEFECTOR
   Objective: To induce elements or individuals of the Cuban military to defect with equipment.
6. Operation BREAK-UP
   Objective: To clandestinely introduce corrosive materials to cause aircraft, vehicle or boat accidents.
7. Operation COVER-UP
   Objective: The objective is to convince the Communist government of Cuba that Naval Forces ostensibly assigned to the MERCURY project is merely a cover.
8. Operation DIRTY TRICK
   Objective: The objective is to provide irrevocable proof that, should MERCURY manned orbit flight fail, the fault lies with the Communists, among them, Cuba.
9. Operation FULL-UP
   Objective: The objective is to destroy confidence in fuel supplied by the Soviet Bloc by indicating it is contaminated.
10. Operation GOOD TIMES
    Objective: To disillusion the Cuban population with Castro image by distribution of fake photographic material.
11. Operation HEAT IS ON
    Objective: To create the impression with Castro Government that certain dyed-in-the-wool Red pilots are planning to defect, thus causing a detrimental tightening of security.
12. Operation INVISIBLE BOMB
    Objective: To create the impression that isolated bombings are taking place in Cuba thus maximizing harassment and confusion of the Castro government.
13. Operation HORN SWOGGLE
    Objective: To crush or force down Cuban MIG aircraft with an all weather intercept capability by communications intrusion.
14. Operation TRUE BLUE
    Objective: To degrade Castro and his government in the eyes of the Cuban people by communication intrusion.
15. Operation PHANTOM
    Objective: The objective is to convince the Castro Government that clandestine penetration and resupply of agents is being regularly conducted.

16. Operation BINGO

Objective: The objective is to create an incident which has the appearance of an attack on the U.S. facilities (GMO) in Cuba, thus providing an excuse for use of U.S. military might to overthrow the current government of Cuba.[11]

Five days later, on February 7, 1962, the Department of Defense made an analysis concerning the risks and the role of the department in relation to the annihilation of communism in Cuba. This analysis based on the following factors:

- Policy of National Security, determined by the NSC during the meeting on May 9, 1961;
- Intelligence estimates on the situation in Cuba;
- The operation on Cuba should be covert, at least in the beginning;
- Time is in favor of Cuba.

It was considered that Cuba represented an increased threat for the United States National Security, and represented a base for the effective expansion of communism in Latin America.

The DOD considered, in perspective, that the USSR could establish ground, sea, or air bases in Cuba and that it also delivered missiles with nuclear warheads to Cuba.

The DOD concluded that the existence of a communist regime in Cuba is incompatible with the minimum of security required for the Western Hemisphere and that the DOD was prepared for openly supporting any popular movement in Cuba to overthrow the communist regime and installing an acceptable government to the United States.

On March 7, 1962, the JCS judged that it was impossible to carry out with success a rebellion inside of Cuba in the next nine or ten months, which would demand from the United States the development of a "provocation" attributed to Cuba to justify a military action on its part.

On March 13, 1962, the DOD and the JCS, represented in the Operations Group of the Caribbean, gave to the Chief of Operations of the Cuba Project (Operation Mongoose) a paper entitled "Justification for a Military Operation in Cuba." In such a paper was accurately and undoubtedly established the implementation of a masked and diversion

---

11. The Joint Chief of Staff, File DOD Representative Caribbean Survey Group, Brigadier General William H. Craig, "Memorandum for Brigadier General Edward G. Landsdale, USAF, Assistant to the Secretary of Defense. Washington, February 2, 1962." Top secret.

plan, as premise for a legitimated provocation, pointing initially to provoke a response from the Cuban part. The actions of harassment and diversion would be given priority to convince the Cubans on an imminent invasion. Therefore, some incidents in or near the Naval Base of Guantánamo were proposed to give credibility in the sense of making responsible and accusing the Cubans for these actions.

The sequence of aggressions would be as follows:

1. To begin dissemination of rumors;

2. To infiltrate Cuban counterrevolutionaries over the fence of the Naval Base of Guantánamo to attack the Base;

3. To capture supposed Cuban saboteurs inside the Base;

4. To initiate turmoil near the main entrance of the Base on the part of the Cuban counterrevolutionaries seeming to be the counterrevolutionaries of the Island;

5. To explode ammunitions in the Base and to start fires;

6. To set fire to aircraft in the Base (sabotage);

7. To launch mortars from outside the Base to inside;

8. To capture assumed assault troops approaching from the sea, or from the vicinity of the Base. To damage facilities;

9. To capture groups simulating militiamen who attack the Base;

10. To sabotage ships in the bay, to start fires of great magnitude;

11. To sink ship at the bay entrance. To make funerals of the supposed victims.

The United States would face these actions through offensive operations to guarantee water supply and electric power, destroying emplacements of artillery and mortars, which threatened the Base.

Another recommendation to justify the military intervention was the creation of an incident "Remember the Maine" type, which might consists in blowing up a U.S. ship in the Bay of Guantánamo and to accuse Cuba; to blow up a U.S. unmanned ship in Cuban waters. The United States would organize the supposed rescue operations of the surviving "crew." A photograph of the victims would be published in the American press, which would provoke a wave of indignation in the American people.

It was also proposed to create a supposed campaign of communist terror in the area of Miami, other cities of Florida and, even, in Washington. It would be indicated that the Cuban émigrés are targets of these campaign; the sinking of a boat with Cubans, traveling to Florida coasts, would be assessed. Bombs would explode in areas chosen in advance, and "Cuban agents" would be under arrest. Faked papers would be elaborated to show Cuba's responsibility. An attack from Cuba and with the

43

support of the Cuban Government and of Fidel Castro, to a neighboring country, mainly in the Caribbean area, would be among these provocations to justify a direct military aggression. Neither was omitted that U.S. pilots manning MIG fighters attacked civil airplanes, assaulted merchant ships and planes of the United States Air Force.

Other additional measures contemplated kidnapping attempts to airplanes and ships promoted by the Cuban Government.

A plan was conceived to create an incident that would show in a completely credible way that an airplane of the Cuban Air Force had shot down a civil airplane, hired and in route from the United States and bound for Jamaica, Guatemala, Panama, or Venezuela. The supposed passengers would be American university students on vacations, or a group of U.S. citizens, with common interests, who had rented the plane.

A last measure to be used as a pretext consisted in structuring an incident in which it was reported that a MIG from the Cuban Air Force had shot down a fighter of the United States Air Force in an unjustified aggression.

In this exposé cannot be omitted the five keys characterizing positions of the DOD in relation to the Operation Mongoose, and that in one way or another they required to be examined from the connection established between the development of the Operation Mongoose and the most complex moment of this scenario: the Cuban Missile Crisis of 1962.

On April 10, 1962, the JCS considered, in a first approach that the so-called Cuban problem should be resolved immediately, while there were no perspectives to destroy the Cuban Revolution from inside or abroad, which demanded the direct U.S. military intervention.

The second approach pointed out that the United States could not tolerate the permanent existence of a communist regime in Cuba because this was a threat to hemispheric security and created conditions for other Latin American nations to follow the Cuban example. The third approach insisted that time was favoring Cuba in its confrontation with the United States, because the Cuban revolutionary state increasingly strengthened its sustaining basis.

The fourth approach proposed a vision extremely dangerous, stating that the United States could undertake a military action on Cuba without risking a general war; while, the conclusion of the fifth approach established the military policy of the Joint Chief of Staff of the United States Armed Forces, when stating that the U.S. military intervention in Cuba was recommended to be undertaken as soon as possible.

In July 1962, the DOD, at request of the Chief of Operations of the Operation Mongoose, Gen. Edward Landsdale, made an assessment on the courses of actions to follow in the United States policy towards Cuba.[12] The assessments were submitted by the representative of the JCS of the DOD, Inspection Group of the Caribbean, Brig. Gen. Benjamin Harris. The variants that the Pentagon proposed concerning possible actions to be followed on Cuba are settled here.

Even though in these analyses undertaken in July 1962—the Operation Mongoose was developing its actions from seven months ago—the impact of Mongoose in the Cuban scenario was not mentioned directly or indirectly, it is evident that the approaches of Brig. Gen. Harris must have been started from a study of the operational situation in Cuba, which, despite the American pledges, was not favorable for his plans and intentions. The proposals of this study were four.

The first proposal was to cancel operational plans, to consider Cuba as a nation of the Bloc and to protect the Hemisphere from this.

According to this proposal, there are two advantages. The first one corresponded with the decrease of the cost of war on Cuba; while the second referred that the United States could present an image of non-intervention in the Hemisphere.

The disadvantages, as to a counterpart, were established according to the parameters inserted in the East-West Conflict, the Cold War, the Contention Doctrine, the Monroe Doctrine, the Manifest Destiny, and the Truman Doctrine. In this way, the disadvantages were identified, Cuba would turn into a communist beachhead in the Western Hemisphere and the United States would be incapable to face the Cuban action in the region. It was considered that this implied to damage the United States prestige and weakened the will to fight on Communism, what was associated, at the same time, with the increase of possibilities of the USSR to establish military bases in the Island. This evidently put in danger the United States national security. Likewise, the United States would be prevented from adopting actions that permitted taking advantage of the leaks that might emerge in the Cuban society. Also, it was the fear that Cuban socialism made firm its achievements and strengthened much more, evidently becoming into a model and example to be followed by other nations of the continent. Therefore, Cuba would feel

12. Paper of the Secretary of Defense Office, Washington 25 D.C., July 23, 1962. The United States National Security Archives. CIHSE Archives.

secure and would become more aggressive in its policy of exporting the Revolution.

In the long run, the United States would have to use enormous financial resources to develop its defensive forces to face the Cuban threat. And finally, this first proposal concluded that tacitly accepting the existence of the Revolution and Communism in Cuba meant the permanent existence of a communist base for subversion and espionage through the Western Hemisphere.

The second proposal comprised to exert all possible diplomatic, economic, and psychological pressure, and of other kind, to overthrow the Castro regime without an overt U.S. military involvement.

The elements in favor of the adoption of this measure were in the fact that the United States would show its adherence to the principle of non-intervention, its respect to the Chart of the UN and the U.S. enunciated policy of not using the force for the solution of conflicts. It was also assessed that according the success of pressures, the United States could save resources and forces.

Five disadvantages were noted concerning this proposal. The first one, in obvious reference to the Kennedy decision of not intervening when the Bay of Pigs, stated that the United States non-intervention policy put into practice since breaking of diplomatic relations on January 3, 1961, had not succeeded. No evident intervention meant not to have undertaken a direct military aggression of the United States Armed Forces in the Island. It was estimated that if applying this via of non-intervention, the Soviets could develop Cuba as a base of operations in the Western Hemisphere and the United States would have to build military bases what would imply enormous expenses in the development of appropriate forms of response. The United States, therefore, would indefinitely have to protect the Hemisphere from the communist threat, and the Revolution would have time in its favor. It is pointed out that this would permit the systematic indoctrination of the youth and reinforcement of the state security and the armed forces. And also, that this would be combined in order to make more remote the hope of an inside revolt in the Island and more expensive the United States military intervention.

The third proposal was aimed at engaging the United States for assisting the Cubans to overthrow the communist regime through phases, step by step, to guarantee success, including the use of the United States military force, if required.

Favorable aspects in the adoption of this way were punctually found in the following considerations: the United States was in conditions to control the schedule of operations on Cuba and would permit a progressive development that might be modified, or concluded according to circumstances; it would make evident the American willingness to backing up anti-Communist forces and to reaffirm the Monroe Doctrine. Also, the United States action would be more acceptable for world opinion, while it would present itself in the role to assist combatants of liberty. A rebellion spread in the Island on the Revolution would simplify some of the problems of the military intervention. The Cuban revolutionary society might be used for subversive goals to spot dissenting elements that might constitute the government of the counterrevolution. By this way, the anti-Communist elements inside and outside the Island would feel encouraged. The economic cost, in terms of military and forces resources, would not be high in accomplishing the support of the counterrevolutionary forces. Finally, the temporary downfall of the Cuban Government would be made sure.

From the angle of the disadvantages various factors were indicated. The time passed in this process would permit a major development of the revolutionary consciousness of the population; likewise, it encloses the danger of foreseeing the coup and warns the Revolutionary Government, which might adopt measures of opportune response, and the possibility to increase the assistance from the Socialist Bloc to Cuba. Another disadvantage referred to the refuse on the part of elements opposed to the military intervention. The use of this third proposal would also require   the United States to use screen-organizations in order to manipulate the counterrevolution; preparing its cadres; developing covert training and operations, which can turn into a complication of national character.

The fourth proposal related to the yearnings and aspirations of the most reactionary sectors of the American right, as well as the counterrevolutionary emigration. This was expressed in the design of using a provocation and overthrowing the Castro regime with the use of the United States military force.

The advantages enunciated comprised aspects related with the possibilities of the U.S. armed forces to undertake actions in the moment and place chosen by the United States. It was also taken into consideration that new revolutionary outbreaks in Latin America would be prevented, and enemy forces of Communism in the world would assess this action as the determination of the United States to face Communism. As important indicated element, it made reference that such action would prove the actuality of the Monroe Doctrine in the context of the inter-American relations; would cut the possibilities to establish Soviet bases in the Island; Cuba, also, would cease as a base of revolutionary subversion in Latin America; and the subsequent deployment of American forces in the region to face the increasing threats of revolutionary process would be prevented.

Among the disadvantages that the action of direct military intervention represented, the possible counterattacks of the USSR in other regions of the world are established; that such a course of action was inconsistent with the Chart of the UN and the non-intervention doctrine agreed at the Bogota Conference.

On August 7, 1962, the subversive strategy of the Central Intelligence Agency against Cuba was reiterated.[13]

The strategy was based on the proposal submitted by the DOD concerning the courses of action against Cuba: "to exert all possible diplomatic, economic, and psychological and other pressures to overthrow the Communist Castro regime without the overt U.S. military commitment."[14] Kennedy would modify this proposal in a way to authorize, if necessary, the direct U.S. intervention. This proposal would be known as the augmented stepped-up Plan B.

The CIA pointed its political actions to the following directions:
- Support to the anti-Cuban activity of the Department of State in the heart of the OAS and in bilateral relations with Latin American states;
- Assisting the Department of State in the formulation of the policy post destruction of the Revolution, the selection of the counter-revolutionary leaders and political groups sponsored by the United States;
- Supporting covertly the Cuban Revolutionary Council and other groups of the counterrevolutionary emigration;
- Seeking ways to make contacts with centers of power of the Cuban government as possible means aimed at splitting the Revolution. The plans of economic war on Cuba increased. The CIA would be involved in the planning of action inter-agencies and in the development of actions. It would also be in charge to undertake, with maximum intensity, sabotage in main industries and public services of the nation (transport, communications and electrical plants) through command operations of special groups. Plans

13. Released paper of the United States National Security Archives. CIHSE Archives.
14. U.S. Department of State, "Memorandum from the Chief of Operations, Operation Mongoose (Landsdale) to the Special Group (Augmented), Attachment," in *Foreign Relations of the United States, 1961-1963*, Volume X, *Cuba 1961-1962* (Washington: U.S. Printing Office, 1997), 901.

to deviate the resources used by the Cuban state in the social and economic development and to have it forced to use them in facing aggressions, were conceived.

The plans of the CIA, concerning the counterrevolution organizations, proposed the reinforcement and fostering of an atmosphere of resistance and revolt of the population in general.

The CIA would also recruit and supply small cells of agents in the main cities and other chosen areas. It would dispose of hideouts for arms, ammunitions, and other supplies in the highest possible amount, in approachable areas for the cells of the resistance, and in potential zones of resistance. The CIA would be the responsible for the supply, covert linking, and communications of leading elements of the counterrevolution before any inside undertaking uprising, as well as to be ready to offer personal and logistic support to the counterrevolutionary organizations and to any inside unleashing uprising.

A plan of aggressions to facilities of the Revolutionary Government, offices of the State Security, militia guards and telephone centers was designed.

Campaigns of propaganda—in the context of the psywar—aimed at praising the Cuban people's will to fight against Communism and to discredit the Cuban Government before the world opinion.

The espionage activity comprised obtaining information on the capabilities of the Cuban government to counteract subversive actions and activities that the bodies of the State Security deployed; activities of the USSR in the Island; the knowledge of the operational situation in the bosom of the counterrevolutionary organizations and the state of mind of the Cuban population. According to these plans, recruitment went to Cubans legally settled in the Island, or in posts of the Cuban government abroad; amongst Cubans living in third countries who travel to other countries through the legal channel; in missions of the government and activity of intelligence addressed against communications of the G-2, the police, and the militia.

In the south of Florida, the CIA would dispose of a powerful radio station, Radio Cuba Libre; balloons of propaganda and leaflets would also be launched. Television broadcastings from Cuba would be interfered from air or sea platforms. The mail channel and the travels of persons going to Cuba would be used to introduce counterrevolutionary propaganda in the country, and activities of anti-Cuban propaganda using scholar groups, professionals, student groupings and others who might be transmitters of subversive messages to their Cuban counterparts would increase.

The CIA should increase its operational personnel on Cuba up to 600 officials and it requested $40 millions for future actions, foreseen for 1963, and $60 millions for 1964.

In the second half of 1962, the DOD assessed the outcomes of a direct U.S. military intervention in the Island. When analyzing Cuba response it was pointed out that the military reaction of Cuba was determined by the will of the FAR—Revolutionary Armed Forces—to resist, of the weapons available and the capability of their use to face the intervention. It was considered that the organization of resistance to an aggression was based on a strong early resistance, followed by the defense of areas previously chosen and the subsequent lengthy guerrilla warfare.

On August 10, 1962, the Special Group (Augmented) (SGA) met in the office of the Secretary of State Dean Rusk, to decide the course of Mongoose after concluding the recollection phase of intelligence, which was about to conclude that month. The Special Group (Augmented) analyzed a plan proposed by John McCone in which actions of limited sabotage were recommended; but President Kennedy demanded a more ambitious plan to destroy the Revolution.

On August 20, 1962, the Chairman of the Special Group (Augmented), Maxwell Taylor, reported to President Kennedy that the Group did not see probability to overthrow the Cuban Government other than the direct U.S. military intervention. Taylor recommended more aggressive plans in the context of Mongoose; and President Kennedy give his authorization, but he specified that no military involvement should be part of these plans.

On August 23, through a National Security Action Memorandum, Kennedy ordered the elaboration of reports that should consider the pros and the cons of a warning statement against the deployment of nuclear weapons in Cuba, and also, the psychological, political, and military effect of such a deployment and the military options the United States can undertake to eliminate the threat. Concerning Operation Mongoose, he gave orders to continue the implementation of the stepped-up Plan B, without public use of the United States Armed Forces, with all possible intensity.[15]

That same day, President Kennedy requested the CIA an estimate of the Soviet personnel transferred to Cuba in recent times, amount of

15. U.S. Department of State, "National Security Action Memorandum No. 181," in *Foreign Relations of the United States, 1961-1963,* Volume X, *Cuba 1961-1962* (Washington: U.S. Printing Office, 1997), 957-958.

the existing Soviet military equipment, its use, and, particularly he was interested to know whether the military constructions, carried out in the Island and related to the installation of SAM missiles, could differ from installations for surface-to-surface missiles.

According to the Director of the CIA, John McCone, the Agency could not distinguish between offensive air-to-surface and surface-to-surface missiles of 350-mile range. The Secretary of Defense, McNamara, insisted that the installation of surface missiles could not be tolerated under any circumstance. Likewise, Kennedy requested the CIA to analyze the danger of threat for the United States, and the effect of missile installation in Cuba for Latin America. He, even, approached the convenience to make a statement in advance in the case the USSR installed missiles in Cuba, and the alternative actions they should undertake before such a situation. In his assessment, McCone told President Kennedy that Cuba was the most serious problem the United States confronted, and that Cuba was the key for Latin America. Besides, if Cuba succeeded, the United States could expect the loss of most Latin American countries.

On August 21, 1962, the DOD had elaborated an action plan for Cuba from some high political aspects, analyzed by the U.S. Government. Amongst the most outstanding elements, the probable arrival of Soviet military personnel to Cuba during July-August, and of many ships with materiel and equipment was underlined.

Also, it was considered as valid the conclusion of the National Board of Estimates that the stepped-up Plan B would not achieve the established objective of destroying from inside the Cuban Revolution. The world opinion was to condemn the United States for these subversive actions, what would result in the loss of prestige for the Kennedy administration. It was evident that the United States was not in conditions to face a new Bay of Pigs.

This recognition—lack of capability to subvert the Revolution from inside—must be taken into consideration when analyzing counterrevolutionary activities in Cuba for the period.

The Cuban Government and the Cuban people had faced, with heroism, all CIA subversive plans. The best Cuba's sons were engaged in a fight to death with imperialism. Some would lose their lives in overt confrontations with CIA and the counterrevolution in cities, rural areas, and coasts; others would be the silent martyrs whose devotion and stoicism are part of the historic memory of the nation.

Aggressions unleashed by agencies specialized in subversion and espionage of the United States Government were to have a high economic cost for the development of the country. Cuba was forced itself, both now and then, to invest enormous economic resources for the defense, from the premise that a revolution is worth so much if it is capable to defend itself. The economic aggressions, sabotage, terrorist actions, paramilitary actions, banditry, and other expressions of subversive activities provoked losses of millions. In the Pentagon assessments for conclusions of the National Board of Estimates, it is added that the stepped-up Plan B would contribute to intelligence, would hinder the Cuban economic development, but this was not enough to prevent advance of the Island because of the USSR solidarity for the Revolution. Even more, it is considered that over time, Cuba would strengthen instead of weakening, and it would turn into a powerful political might in Latin America. There was also the fear that Cuba would become a possible base for the installation of middle-range ballistic missiles (MRBM) and of installations where communications of the defensive system of the United States, including space defensive system, would be controlled. Therefore, the DOD elaborated recommendations to carry out a more aggressive line on Cuba; it is clear that Mongoose was not fulfilling the proposed objectives.

Then, it was considered necessary to undertake deeper political actions: systematic and aggressive actions to move and alarm all Latin America and the world concerning the supposed dangers that Cuba meant. These actions required the United States press involvement and other countries assistance in propaganda campaigns; the use of the UN, the OAS, through contacts with capitalistic countries at level of heads of States, Foreign Ministers, embassies, private or half-public organizations, such as young groupings, agrarian cooperatives, labor, and religious organizations, etc.

It was proposed the involvement of the United States Armed Forces to occupy the Island, to destroy the Revolution, and to establish a friendly government to the United States interests. All actions inside the Operation Mongoose remained, and the necessity of the stepped-up Plan B to overthrow the Cuban Revolutionary Government was reiterated.

In response to Kennedy decision to continue a more aggressive program of covert actions on Cuba, the CIA began to elaborate a list of sabotage targets in Cuba for the Special Group (Augmented).

On October 4, 1962, the SGA met for discussing the progress of the Operation Mongoose. Robert Kennedy expressed that the president was concerned with the progress of the Operation Mongoose. He believed that to the mounting of sabotage operations should be given more priority. The SGA agreed a plan for mining the Cuban seaports. On October 15, the SGA met again to order the acceleration of covert operations on Cuba.

On October 16, Robert Kennedy referred again the John F. Kennedy's position when arguing the general discontent of president Kennedy with the evolution of the Operation Mongoose. Different alternatives to eliminate missile bases, recently spotted in the Island, were discussed.

On October 22, the Cuban Missile Crisis, which would have repercussions in Mongoose destiny, began.

On October 30, the United States Government broke up all operations of Task Force W, CIA operational group in charge of covert operations on Cuba, in the program of the Operation Mongoose. The Chief of the Task Force W, William K. Harvey, had sent, on his own, two infiltration teams to the Island in order to carry out sabotage and intelligence actions in the middle of the Cuban Missile Crisis. The revolutionary forces captured one of these teams in the Cuban territory. By late October, Harvey planed sending another team for special missions, but one of the operational elements reported Robert Kennedy about this project, who ordered McCone the cessation of all these operations. The Chief of Operations, Operation Mongoose, was sent to Florida to check the conclusion of such subversive project.

THE OPERATION MONGOOSE: ITS IMPACT IN CUBA. SETBACK OF SUBVERSIVE PLANS ON THE REVOLUTION: CAUSES AND EFFECTS

The U.S. Intelligence Community proposed themselves the organization and restoration of the counterrevolution in the country after designing their new subversive strategy about Cuba exposed in the Program Mongoose.

The *modus operandi* consisted in creating an internal opposition movement to the Revolution, capable to unleash, by itself, a counter-revolutionary-armed insurrection. This would create the ideal political conditions to make sure the last proposal of Mongoose: the direct military intervention of the United States Armed Forces and the destruction of the Revolution.

In their assessments, experts of Mongoose did not recognize the social, and economic achievements, and the development of the political culture accomplished by the Revolution in only three years.

The creation of a modern and generalized health system—completely free—, the Literacy Campaign, the eradication of unemployment, and the advances achieved in agriculture since the first Agrarian Reform in 1959 proved to be the inexpugnable strength of the Revolution.

The patriotic spirit, the conquest of political sovereignty and the economic independence, strengthened the revolutionary ideology of the people, willing to defend Socialism to its last consequences.

For analyzing and interpreting how Mongoose is seen in the theater of operations, it is important to underline different aspects that, in our opinion, were related with the roots, development, and ending of Mongoose. It meant a new Bay of Pigs for Kennedy administration, but this time the failure remained silent, in the limits of the secret war on Cuba. Kennedy did not have to explain to the nation the dimension of this defeat; neither was it necessary to invoke the National Security doctrine to justify undertaken actions, nor assuming the direct responsibility of the outcome of the Operation. Even though the end of Mongoose opened a new chapter in the Kennedy administration policy, for experts in the United States National Security, it would not mean, of course, the search, in terms of Realpolitik, of a truly fair and rational solution of those problems present in the historic conflict between both nations to allow the development of normal relations between both states, according to the principles of international law.

The actions undertaken by the CIA and other intelligence agencies in Cuba in 1962, require to be examined in the light of the following elements:

1. Making decisions in relation to operations and actions to develop in Cuba did not correctly estimate the existing operational-and-political situation and operational-and-ideological in Cuba, that is, it did not conveniently assessed the scenario, with objectivity and veracity.

It is undeniable that the aggressions promoted on the Revolution resulted in enormous damages in human lives and properties. It is estimated that from January to August 1962, more than 5000 terrorist actions and sabotage took place; among them, 600 of certain magnitude.

The sabotage activity comprised burning cane-fields, and schools opened by the Revolution; destruction of agricultural and industrial productive facilities; bombing cane-fields with white phosphorus from small planes coming from the United States; putting transport means out of action; setting fire the houses of revolutionary families and attacking cooperatives.

The April-24-1962 sabotage to a construction facility of the National Bank, on Belascoaín and San Lázaro Streets in La Habana; the

54

fire of a chemical-manure warehouse of the INRA (Agrarian Reform National Institute) in Cotorro; the contamination of a sugar cargo bound for the USSR, on August 22, 1962, while the ship carrying the cargo was in San Juan, Puerto Rico, for maintenance, are amongst the examples.

According to figures given by the Analysis and Information Department of the Ministry of the Interior, there were 4000 cane-field fires in 1962.

But it is also important to underline—and here experts in issues of security agree, both the ones who faced Mongoose and the ones who executed the Operation—that Mongoose could not fulfill the objectives it had been conceived for, because the CIA did not have the operational capability to direct and instruct the Program Mongoose; the Cuban socialist society exerted its hegemony through the revolutionary state, which had eliminated the political and economic might of the Cuban dependent bourgeoisie in 1960 and 1961.

What social group or class could the counterrevolution sustain on for organizing and restructuring itself? What acceptable messages could the counterrevolutionary organizations offer to the revolutionary masses inside or outside Cuba? What political program could the counterrevolutionary organizations—Revolutionary Recovery Movement (MRR), People's Revolutionary Movement (MRP), Student Revolutionary Directorate (DRE), Christian-Democratic Movement (MDC), November-30 Movement (M-30-11), Liberation Armed Forces (FAL), Anti-Communist Civic Resistance (RCA; counterrevolutionary organization bloc), Rescue and other organizations—to be manipulated by CIA in the operational theater during Mongoose for the Cuban people as an alternative to the Revolution? What counterrevolutionary organization operated independently of the CIA in 1962, with own political personality? Were not all organizations, and without exception, pro-American, neo-annexionist, anti-Communist, and were all yoked by the most conservative sectors of a Church whose hierarchy had become a political party of the counterrevolution in 1959-1961, not de jure but de facto, without having listened the honest voices of believers, some secular people and some clergies who supported the revolution of the humble, by the humble, and for the humble, which had expelled the merchants of the capitalistic temple?

And back to the making of decisions, an aspect that sometimes is not taken into consideration can always be pointed out. This aspect refers to the psychology of human beings who, in the Chief of Staff of Mongoose, organized the actions on Cuba.

The expert in counter-insurgency, Edward Landsdale, knew the insurgent movements in Asia, but he was not an expert in revolutions. He was deeply ignorant of the psychology of Cuban revolutionaries, the Cuban reality, and Cuba capability to respond to his project.

The Kennedys needed a revenge to bring U.S. back the Bay of Pigs stroke. For them, Mongoose was a vendetta on the Cuban nation and the politician who had revealed the United States purposes, south of Río Grande. More than a target for the U.S. intelligence services, Cuba had become an obsession for the United States, and work on Cuba demanded a scientific reasoning, without passion and emotion. The decisions were not accurate because they lack a view sustained on correct estimates, or in the underestimation of the correct intelligence estimates.[16]

2. The counterrevolutionary organizations inland could not systematically operate, they lacked a strong unity to integrate them; they never achieved establishing an effective organic connection with terrorist groups which operated at the Escambray Mountains, main spot of rural counterrevo-lution in the country.[17]

The counterrevolutionary actions did not achieve, at any place, disposing of popular support; they were simultaneously repudiated and faced by the State Security mechanism and revolutionary organizations. Significantly, it is also necessary to point out that they lacked effective counter-intelligence mechanism to foresee penetration of security agents. In 1962, the bodies of the Cuban security, according to a CIA released document, penetrated almost all counterrevolutionary organizations.

A factor to be taken into account in the study of the counterrevolution in 1962 is the lack of a leadership capable to integrate, join, achieve the cohesion of, and lead the counterrevolutionary organizations. Not even Miró Cardona, Antonio Varona, Justo Carrillo, or Manuel Ray, to mention some, possessed the required political attributes to lead a political movement against the Revolution. They were figures of the Cuban traditional policy of the period before 1959, simple instruments of the White

---

16. The consulted literature makes us infer that the prevailing views corresponded to proposals for the acceleration of the subversive program on Cuba. In the Program Mongoose, views of the Executive (John F. Kennedy and his advisors), the Pentagon, the Central Intelligence Agency, the State Department, and the structures of the National Security Council in charge of the Cuban case (Counter-insurgency Group, and Special Group Augmented) were present.

17. Central Intelligence Agency, *Handbook of Counterrevolutionary Organizations,* 1962. Released paper. CIHSE Archives.

House, jokers of the counterrevolution. If the directorate of the counter-revolution based outside of Cuba in the form of the Cuban Revolutionary Council (in appearance) and in the JM-WAVE Station in Florida (the truly headquarters of the counterrevolution in the United States), clandestine structures of the counterrevolution inland could neither have initiative and creativity in their deployment, nor draw their own strategic and tactic guidelines.

3. The measures adopted by the Unites States Government on Cuba, in the period prior 1962, reverted against the Mongoose objectives.

The breaking of diplomatic relations in January 1961 meant the loss of a very important base for the execution of subversive activities, because when the embassy was withdrawn, the station installed there vanished. On one hand, the CIA was forced to transfer some of the tasks executed in the center to other intelligence agencies operating from legal positions.[18] On the other hand, the United States Government had encouraged the emigration of professionals, technicians, and specialists with the purpose to bleed the economy of the Revolution white. Together with these, elements affected by revolutionary acts (bourgeoisie and small bourgeoisie) also emigrated, who joined to other early émigrés of the counterrevolution: the *Batistianos*.[19] Thus, the CIA lost important cadres for the recruitment of counterrevolutionary forces inland. Although the intention was to damage the Revolution abroad, a purpose not fulfilled in fact, the counterrevolution in Cuba experienced a process of abandonment and frustration.

In this sense, the economic measures aimed at creating and establishing a tightened economic blockade—initiated in the Eisenhower administration and subsequently followed by Kennedy—could not strangle the Cuban economy. The decisive and immediate support of the USSR and other countries of the Socialist Bloc allowed Cuba to guarantee the functioning of industry and agriculture. The Cuban foreign trade was restructured and a new economic order was structured, based on the socialist planning.

---

18. In this sense we should consider that is presumable that the CIA: a) aimed its work at increasing its activity with illegal officials of deep cover, foreseeing the breaking of relations; b) increased its recruiting activity in the country to leave "moles"; c) froze operations in development, initiated by the legal station. In 1962, the illegal channel of penetration was the fundamental way that the CIA used on Cuba. In subsequent years it was to be the same.

19. Followers of Fulgencio Batista, Cuba's President and dictator before 1959. *Ed.*

So, instead of provoking the long awaited social chaos and political crisis—indispensable conditions to generate succeeding subversive actions—, the people became more conscious of the significance of the threats and objectives of the U.S. imperialism against the Island.

4. In order to establish the phases characterizing the enemy activity in 1962 in our territory, we can establish the following periodization:
- First half of 1962;
- July-August 1962;
- August 1962 until the immediate period after the Cuban Missile Crisis of 1962.

In the first half of 1962, the CIA proposed, first of all, the restructuring of the counterrevolutionary movement inland. The organization chosen to undertake this action was the MRR. At the CIA released papers it is explained that this agency considered the MRR the one of highest confidence and operational capability.

In January 1962, the agent of the CIA political action, Manuel Guillot Castellanos, was infiltrated. His activity was aimed at explaining the content, objectives, and purposes of Mongoose in Cuba during this phase:
- To achieve unity of the counterrevolutionary organizations in the country, thus creating conditions for a general uprising in Cuba;
- To link the counterrevolutionary movement with armed groups at the Escambray;
- To establish a bloc of organizations under someone's command, with his aid and radar operator at province level;
- To exfiltrate national leaders of the main counterrevolutionary organizations to form a provisional board of government for propaganda activity and other political activities;
- The CIA would guide every bloc of province counterrevolutionary organization.

Manuel Guillot Castellanos could not fulfill the mission assigned. Months later, in May 1962, during a new infiltration, the bodies of the State Security captured him, together with other leaders of the MRR and other counterrevolutionary organizations.

In addition to CIA agent of political action, Guillot was military coordinator of the MRR in the United States, and his attempt to forge the unity of the counterrevolutionary organizations MRR, MRP, DRE, and the M-30-11 organization was a complete failure. The MRR suffered a demolishing stroke in the country. Its main leader in Cuba, Juan Falcón Zanmar, was also under arrest. In order to know MRR plans in

Cuba in this phase, Manuel Guillot Castellanos statements are illustrative.[20]

In the period July-August 1962, the CIA reactivated its subversive mechanism for the plan of general uprising scheduled for October of that year, according to the schedule in the Program Mongoose, approved by the United States President.

In this phase, the Liberation Anti-Communist Front (FAL) would execute the counterrevolutionary plot.[21] Such organization was created by mid-1962; Francisco Evelio Pérez Menéndez was appointed ringleader, and Manuel Silió Matos was the chief of military operations in La Habana. The FAL headquarter planned a general uprising for August 30, 1962. In order to undertake its plans, the FAL made the coordination with the counterrevolutionary organizations Revolutionary Unit, Rescue, Second Front and M-30-11.

A study of the uprising plan reveals the following elements of operational interest:

- The general uprising would cover the whole Republic;
- The signal of such a plan would be a blackout at 22:00 hrs, on August 30, 1962. At the moment, the members of the FAL, with black uniforms, would seize police stations and small military and militia units in different zones and boroughs of the country, but mainly in Havana city; according to the structure of the organization, the police stations would be seized by zone heads;
- The civil part of the FAL, assisted by members of other organizations, would bloc the capital city with cars, buses, and trucks, which would be set on fire to hinder the traffic of military transport;
- Supposedly, the FAL had elements in its ranks from the electric company who would blow up Tallapiedra electric plant;
- The facilities to seize were: the General Chief of Staff of the FAR, the Naval Sanitary warehouse, the Rancho Boyeros Airport, the Mariel Naval Academy, the Maritime Training Academy, Barlovento and Casablanca towns.
- Also they would try to seize different units of the Revolutionary Navy, in which some elements of the FAL were infiltrated, to distribute arms among civil elements.

20. Statement of Manuel Guillot Castellanos. CIHSE Archives.
21. Record of counterrevolutionary organizations. CIHSE Archives.

For the uprising, scheduled for August 30, 1962, the leadership of the FAL had created a specialized unit in charge of undertaking sabotage and attempts to crime against lives of leaders of the Revolution. The Chief of Staff of the FAL would settle in the former Trelles School and at the Junior High School in El Vedado.

The day before the uprising, the bodies of the State Security, which had penetrated this activity, arrested the leadership of the FAL and elements plotted in this action.

The reviewed papers allow to state that during the FAL plan, the CIA was involved and the Naval Intelligence Agency of the Naval Base of Guantánamo collaborated.

A subsequent assessment undertaken by the CIA, contained in the *Handbook of Counterrevolutionary Organizations in Cuba* (released paper), 1962, concluded that agents of the Cuban State Security had penetrated the FAL.

The annihilation of the FAL was a serious setback for CIA plans; the Agency, however, continued with its plans to reorganize the counterrevolution within Cuba. With these purposes, the RCA emerged in September, made up of different counterrevolutionary groups. The plan designed by this organization, headed by Luis David Rodríguez (national leader of the MRR in Cuba), was aimed at promoting again an uprising within Cuba. A group of actions was established, which was a self-provocation at the Naval Base of Guantánamo through the use of command groups trained in a training facility in New Orleans. The beginning of this self-provocation would agree at the same time with supposed attacks the RCA was to unleash against important economic targets and military facilities associated to a plan of attempts to crime against the life of the Commander in Chief, Fidel Castro. In order to make sure these actions, the RCA was supported by the Naval Intelligence Agency of the Base, and by the counterrevolutionary group Revolutionary Rescue, headed from the United States by the CIA agent Tony Varona, who had the backing of the American mob. The CIA, of course, was in the center of this operation. The events arisen as a result of the Cuban Missile Crisis postponed the execution of this plan.

Subsequently, in March 1963, the principal ringleaders of the RCA were arrested, their armament seized, and the plot to assassinate the Commander in Chief, to be executed on March 13, 1963, frustrated.

If the annihilation of the Western United Front (FUO) meant the end of CIA attempts to form a big intelligence and subversion network in Cuba, within the context of the Program Mongoose, the annihilation of the RCA was the final stroke for plans aimed at reorganizing the counterrevolution within Cuba. The RCA plans had been ambitious: terrorist actions, sabotage and coordination with the leadership of terrorist groups at the Escambray, internal uprising, and attempts to crime plans. The RCA collapse ends a chapter of the counterrevolution in Cuba. The Central Intelligence Agency had lost its men of higher confidence, preparation and expertise. The desirable fifth column for the invasion had been dismantled; the CIA operational resources in the counterrevolutionary structures could not recover from that demolishing stroke. The counterrevolution could not be exported to Cuba. The people in revolution proved one more time, its capability to counteract and overcome the enemy activity. They were men of cold mind, clean hands and ardent hearts who were on the vanguard of this secret war against the CIA.

The counterrevolution finally moved to the United States. Florida was to become the Mecca of terrorism, espionage, sabotage plans and attempts to crime, ideological-and-political subversion, and paramilitary actions. The counterrevolution was to melt with CIA macabre terrorist projects to develop in the United States from the failure of Mongoose to date. Evidences and proofs of all and every covert operation undertaken by the CIA on our country are at the Cuban Revolution secret archives. Enemy propaganda means cannot adulterate history of this hidden, silent, and heroic war, written with blood, sweat, and abnegation. The truth is always revolutionary, and always prevails in life and science. If something is evident is that the counterrevolution was manipulated, used according to convenience and interests of the United States policy, trained and financed by that country, and which never had a own entity to generate its subversive projects.

CHAPTER III. The Clandestine Empire of the CIA: The JM-WAVE Station

In the middle of the '50s, the Central Intelligence Agency established offices in different American states. One of these facilities was in Miami.

The proximity to the Caribbean, Central and South America, facilitated intelligence activity to the officials of the headquarters who 1500 kilometers away, had to make that trip to contact their agents in transit through the south of the United States. Likewise, the increasingly presence of commercial firms, capital investment of Latin America and the Caribbean, and the development and increase of immigrants from those countries opened important operational possibilities for the CIA that proposed removing the FBI in the direction of intelligence operations in the region.

The CIA Station in Miami, in the own American territory, had specific organization characteristics. It was directly subordinated to the Western Hemisphere Division of the Directorate of Plans of the CIA Headquarters, and worked in these conditions as a CIA Station in overseas. Initially, the station disposed of a small payroll of officials, most experienced ones and about to retire, who had fulfilled missions outside the United States.

From different sources, it is known that the CIA Station in Florida tracked the Cuban revolutionary process to obtain an accurate and objective knowledge of the political situation in the Island, particularly, the armed struggle in the mountains. When the Revolution took power on January 1, 1959, the Florida station acquired a high operational significance in the conspiracy plans on Cuba. With the preparations of Operation Zapata (Pluto), approved by President Eisenhower on March 17, 1960, the payroll of the station, which was developing complex missions against the stability of the Cuban revolutionary power, notably increased.

When losing its legal station in Havana and the operational base in Santiago de Cuba, with the breaking of diplomatic relations with Cuba, decreed by the Dwight D. Eisenhower Government on January 3, 1961, the CIA Headquarters had to immediately reinforce the activity of its station in Miami.

From the defeat at the Bay of Pigs, and with the arrival of the Operation Mongoose in November 1961, this station, baptized with the name-code of JM-WAVE, was to become into the principal instrument of CIA subversion, terrorism, and intelligence on Cuba. Coincidentally, the unit of the Headquarters in charge of Cuba, was hoisted to the rank of a Sub-Division (Cuban Task Force), and all activities on the Island, which the different legal stations developed, sending specialists elsewhere to coordinate operations of the anti-Cuban mechanism of the Agency, were directed from there.

In these brief lines, the backgrounds of the JM-WAVE Station, whose sinister history is jealously kept in the secret vaults of an office located in Langley, Virginia, are summed up.

In order to undertake Mongoose plans, Kennedy administration decided to make changes in the principal commands of the Central Intelligence Agency, which had been directly and mainly involved in the failed Operation Pluto, ending with the defeat of the Bay of Pigs invasion.

On November 28, 1961, Allen Dulles's career as the CIA Director was to end, after eight years in charge of the agency, with a broad curriculum in the field of covert operations since the times when he participated in the clandestine activities of the Office for Strategic Services (OSS) during the World War II. Because of his contribution to the United States defense, President John F. Kennedy decorated him with the National Security Order. Then, he was appointed advisor for historic research of the Agency. His departure meant the first restructuring that CIA was to experience since its foundation; it was the signal of new faces in Langley, willing to carry out the Kennedys' policy in the crusade against Communism, from a new strategic vision announced by the Taylor Commission after assessing causes and conditions of the Bay of Pigs failure.

Then, the chairman of the Atomic Energy Commission since 1958, John McCone, was to replace Dulles in his post, intelligent decision of Kennedy to choose a Republican for this post, without any prior direct link with CIA operations.

The CIA Deputy Director Charles Cabell was replaced by Gen. Marshall Carter. Gen. Maxwell Taylor, close collaborator of Kennedy, one of the main architects in the design of Operation Mongoose, held the post of Chief of the JCS. The chief of the powerful clandestine services of the Agency and right arm of Dulles in all CIA covert operations, Richard Bisell, was bound for the Institute for Defense Analysis, a center of military studies.

In February 1962, Richard Helms was to be appointed as the new chief of the CIA clandestine services, replacing Richard Bisell. He, a man associated to the Agency since its foundation, had not significantly been directly involved in the plans of Operation Pluto on Cuba.

In the specific field of operations on Cuba during Mongoose, the new CIA directorate appointed William Harvey as Chief of the Cuban Task Force (Task Force W), in charge of overseeing and controlling operations on Cuba from its headquarters in Langley. With a broad record in clandestine operations on the USSR in Berlin, Harvey was not by any chance also the Chief of the CIA Executive Action Unit, known as ZR-Rifle, since its creation in 1961. The program of CIA executive actions was carrying out the assassination of enemy political figures, hostile to the United States interests from the principle of the plausible denial that should mask, in all moments, the United States Government involvement in the undertaking of political assassinations.

The second in command in the Cuban Task Force was to be Samuel Halpern, who would play an important role in the CIA operations, mounted in 1963 in the Multi-Track Program as second chief of the Special Affairs Section, commanded by Desmond FitzGerald.

In his intervention during the scholar conference, "Bay of Pigs: 40 Years Later," held in Havana in March 2001, Halpern, who attended as member of the delegation of his country, diminished importance to the political and operational dimension of Operation Mongoose. He expressed that the CIA did not devise this strategy, and made the Kennedy administration responsible for having planned, organized, and executed such a strategy, justifying the Agency involvement. Forty years later the Agency does not want the word Mongoose to be mentioned in public, nor incorporating this as an important chapter of the history of aggressions of the CIA and the counterrevolution on the Cuban nation.

To direct the JM-WAVE Station, considered by an American author as the CIA clandestine empire, William K. Harvey chose Theodore Shackley, man of confidence associated to the covert activities of the former against Eastern-Europe countries. The second chief of the JM-WAVE was Gordon Campbell, who was in charge of naval operations of the groups that executed paramilitary operations, infiltration in or exfiltration from the Island.

Why did Langley decide to turn the JM-WAVE Station, in practice, into a special CIA Deputy Directorate in charge in carrying out its operations on Cuba? How was the JM-WAVE Station structured? Who made up its working staff? What impact did the JM-WAVE relations have with the Kennedy administration plans against Cuba? What repercussion did the JM-WAVE existence produce in the subsequent United States political life?

The Task Force W, under direction of William K. Harvey was indeed subordinated to the CIA Western Hemisphere Division, the same as Western Hemisphere 4 was subject to the control of the Chief of the CIA clandestine services Richard Helms, but at the same time, it was overseen by the Special Group (Augmented) of the National Security Council and by the Chief of Operations, Operation Mongoose, Gen. Edward Landsdale, emblematic figure for the Kennedys because of his involvement in counter-insurgency in the Philippines and the Indochina Peninsula. In this sense, it is important to underline the role that Robert Kennedy played in the control and supervision of the JM-WAVE tasks. From its beginning and until its final end, the Operation Mongoose was a Kennedy project whose main actors were President Kennedy, Gen. Maxwell Taylor, the Attorney General Robert Kennedy, and Gen. Edward Landsdale, as well as the main president's advisors.

The Operation Mongoose was assigned to the CIA as a strategic mission of national security, as a main objective of the United States foreign policy for Latin America and the Caribbean, and one of the essential objectives of the West-East Conflict. For the United States, the annihilation of the Cuban Revolution meant to guarantee its example not to spread; that other countries did not go through the way of the revolutionary struggle, the anti-imperialism, and why not?, through a new Socialism emerged from the own historical, economic, social, and cultural conditions that Cuba was about to expose in the Second Havana Declaration in February 1962.

All these considerations are the reasons for the deployment of forces and means used in the *modus operandi* of the JM-WAVE Station. According to the United States released papers, after officially approving the Operation Mongoose on November 30, 1961, the mechanism of this station experienced big changes, up to the Kennedy administration aspirations.

It is not feasible to specify the budget assigned for the Operation. The sources consulted, from released papers to studies undertaken by experts in national security, differ. There are some that calculate the budget for 1962 as high as $50, or $100 millions. Any figure in this scale can be estimated. In addition to its specific budget, Mongoose expenses were under control of different organizations involved in this project: the CIA, the DOD, the State Department, the USIA, the Treasure Department and other specialized agencies of the intelligence community, and secretariats and departments of the U.S. Government.

Consulted studies allow calculating that at the JM-WAVE Station, about 600 CIA officials were operating, and that at the JM-WAVE payroll, between 3000 and 4000 collaborators of Cuban origin were registered.

In order to have an approximate calculus of the magnitude of the forces that intervened in Mongoose, let us say that on October 10, 1962, in a CIA released report it is pointed out that there were 415 counter-revolutionary organizations, including the ones operating in the Island and the United States. The JM-WAVE analysts considered that there were 371 counterrevolutionary groups and organizations.

In the center of reception at Opa Locka, the CIA recruited its agents and collaborators in Florida.

In every CIA important legal station abroad, there was at least a CIA case officer in charge of actions of the Program Mongoose in that country. These actions were coordinated with the JM-WAVE Station in Florida. In Latin America, Mexico City was a top priority plaza. The Chief of operations in that city was David Atlee Phillips. Spain and the Federal German Republic were strong CIA working plazas against Cuba.

With the beginning of Mongoose, the Coral Gables unit was transferred to the Richmond air-sea station, in the outskirts of south of Miami, which had been handed over by the United States Navy to the Miami University for field research and developing plans. It was the south campus of the university, which, on its part, had facilitated these terrains to the CIA for its non-scientific and non-scholar use. The buildings of the Zenith Technical Enterprises Inc. would appear, that immediately the CIA was to use as a cover to justify its presence in that place.

In an extension of 1571 acres (approximately 6.4 sq km) there were wooden buildings for the JM-WAVE offices and warehouses, whose real identity was unknown—at least officially—for the rector of Miami University. The Zenith Technical Enterprises Inc. was prepared with all characteristics of commercial business: sale ads and fake commercial licenses were hanging on the walls, while guards dressed in grey uniforms watched the restricted zones.

The JM-WAVE, in its genesis, violated the principles that founded the creation of the CIA, that is, not to develop intelligence operations and others of national interest in or towards inland.

In the city of Miami, an intricate infrastructure was established in order to operationally make sure and supply actions on Cuba to be developed from the JM-WAVE. Tour agencies, armories, sport-item shops, real-estate firms, and private-detective agencies offered services and coverage for the station staff.

There were weapons of different kind, brands, coming from any part of the world in the warehouses. Polygraphy and psychology specialists, as well as physicians made up the payroll of the station. Dozens of apartments and luxurious mansions were registered as properties of the Zenith Technical Enterprises Inc., which were used as contact places. Training centers for commands of special operations were located in different keys near the coast. The swamp region of the Everglades was also used for these goals; even the JM-WAVE had achieved establishing here a training center with the appearance of a Hunting Club.

The station disposed of different planes, naval means including mother and supply ships, speed boats, and rubber rafts to infiltrate and exfiltrate agents towards and from Cuba; to undertake deposits of weapons and supplies for counterrevolutionary organizations inland. There was a small maritime base in Coral Gables.

Experts in political actions were in charge of their cases and delivered huge amounts of financial resources to privileged elements in the counterrevolutionary emigration. This meant that the funds were to be bound for those organizations, which completely fulfilled the indications of their case officials.

The Foreign Information Section was looking for and obtaining economic and political information about events in Cuba relying in sources of the counterrevolutionary emigration and agents in the Island. Generally, the quality of the information to be obtained from the leaders of the Revolution was, however, poor and scanty. Still today, there is no information to allow us to assure that the information-and-analysis staff of the JM-WAVE warned Washington about the presence of atomic missiles in Cuban soil; there are, nevertheless, different hypotheses concerning this. Some indicate that Cuban refugees interviewed at Opa Locka offered data, between September and October, on the presence of missiles in the Pinar del Río Province; others indicate that members of an intelligence network operating in Cuba obtained information prior the flight of the U-2 on October 14, 1962. Warren Frank, who had been the first substitute of Shackley when the latter was working at the Czechoslovakia Bureau of the CIA, was at the head of this section.

In the JM-WAVE, there were, also, Security, Counterintelligence, and Communications sections.

The Instruction Division trained groups to undertake infiltration and exfiltratrion in the Island.

The paramilitary groups, in charge of special operations, operated as part of clandestine services. These were located outside the JM-WAVE headquarters, in different security houses. William (Rip) Robertson, who had an active involvement in the mercenary invasion at the Bay of Pigs, was among the heads of these groups. Grayston Lynch, the American man with major hierarchy who was involved in the Assault Brigade 2506 at the Bay of Pigs, was another head of the paramilitary groups. Robert Wall, a specialist in guerrilla warfare, with expertise acquired in Malaysia, was in charge of infiltration teams, while Justin Gleichauf was the responsible of the small branch of the station, located in Downtown Miami.

Rocky Farnworth had directed—prior Mongoose—the Covert Operations Section of the JM-WAVE. He, after disagreeing with Shackley for having views and working styles quite different from the methods, forms, and manner to develop covert operations, was replaced by David Morales, a close collaborator of David Atlee Phillips in the secret war of CIA on Arbenz administration in Guatemala, 1954. Subsequently, David was an official of the CIA legal station in Havana, where he met many CIA agents who collaborated with the JM-WAVE and who were ringleaders of counterrevolutionary organizations settled in the United States, or operating in Cuba.

Executive actions were another main direction of activity that was gestating at the station, that is, in plain and accurate language: the planning of political assassinations. The actors of these plans not only were the CIA, its Cuban agents and the counterrevolutionary organizations.

In order to camouflage much more its goals and to orient its activity to false targets, the Executive Actions Unit, ZR-Rifle, rested on the American mob for undertaking attempts to crime against the main leaders of the Revolution, particularly Fidel Castro—even though also included Raúl Castro and Ernesto "Che" Guevara—, in collaboration with the counterrevolutionary organizations.

In the Cura-Manco[1] case, undertaken by the Bodies of the State Security in the '60s, papers of these plans exist, as well as official papers of the United States Government released by the Select Committee of the U.S. Senate in 1975, and in the Report of the Inspector General of 1967 on the CIA plots to assassinate Fidel Castro. This case was executed against the CIA agents Ramón and Leopoldina Grau Alsina, main actors of the Peter Pan Operation.

In his condition as the JM-WAVE Director, Shackley made contacts with representatives of the mob through William Harvey to support these actions.

In order to execute tasks in which it was necessary to preserve at maximum the cover of the JM-WAVE, it rested on a clandestine structure arisen during the Operation Pluto in 1961: Operation 40. According to information existing in the archives of the Ministry of the Interior (MININT), the Operation 40 aimed at being the repressive body of the Assault Brigade 2506, once this had strengthened positions in the Cuban territory after landing.

The Operation 40 was created to seize the archives of the Cuban Security; to occupy the main bodies of the State central administration, particularly, the armed institutions, the key economic centers; and to arrest the main leaders of the Revolution. The men of such operation could not step on Cuban soil. When invaders of the Assault Brigade were defeated at the Bay of Pigs, the landing plan of the unit was changed by the retreat to Florida.

In that sense, the elements of the Operation 40 were acting as intermediaries between the JM-WAVE and terrorist groups of Cuban origin in U.S. territory, with which the CIA was not interested to have direct contacts, and which were involved in weapons traffic from Dallas and New Orleans. Thus, terrorists were supplied with money, weapons and equipments, and received instructions for undertaking missions that the JM-WAVE headquarters planned.

The connection of the Operation 40 with the American mob—extremely interested in retrieving its lost paradise in Havana with the arrival of the Revolution—could not be absent in these actions. The main members of the Operation 40, headed by Joaquín Sanjenis, one of the police leaders of the Carlos Prío Socarrás administration, and trained by the FBI, came from the repressive corps of Batista dictatorship. They had been collaborators of the FBI or the CIA before the triumph of the Revolution.

1. It means Priest-One-handed person. *Ed.*

CHAPTER IV. The Covert Operations during the Operation Mongoose

ARMED INFILTRATIONS FROM U.S. TERRITORY

In the context of the Operation Mongoose, the use of the illegal channel was indispensable to undertake intelligence, subversive, terrorist and operational logistics plans. Since the CIA did not have a legal station in Cuba, the illegal channel was the most appropriate way to export counterrevolution to Cuba.

According to research carried out to date, based on information from the MININT archives, 42 infiltrations of significant character have been reported in the national territory in 1962, in which 117 CIA agents intervened.

Infiltrations were as follows: January was the most affected month with ten; February with one; March with four; April and May with six each one; June with three; October with five; and December with seven, for a total of forty-two infiltrations; in July, August, and November no fact of this kind was reported.[1]

The purposes of these infiltrations were aimed at:
- To deliver and supply weapons to terrorist groups in the main mountain regions of the country (Las Villas, Pinar del Río, and Oriente

---

1. This information rested on data supplied by the General Directorate of the Border Troops and research studies of the CIHSE (Senior Researcher José Luis Méndez, Ph. D., and Researcher Pedro Etcheverry).

provinces) and to counterrevolutionary organizations operating in the Island.

- To undertake sabotage actions in key economy sectors previously chosen by the CIA Task Force, with the approval of the Special Group (Augmented) of the United States National Security Council.
- To undertake activities for searching and obtaining information in order to know possible zones for future rebellion, and know military information on the FAR facilities and the Soviet military presence in different locations of the Cuban territory.
- To contact with different counterrevolutionary groups and organizations in order to achieve their unity; to exert control over them and to assure direction mechanisms of the counterrevolution.
- To infiltrate and to exfiltrate agents to carry out specific operations related with intelligence, subversion and supply activity.
- To introduce technical means for communications station-agent and agent-station.
- To create new counterrevolutionary focuses in the former Oriente and Las Villas provinces. In Oriente Province, the Naval Base of Guantánamo, played a determinant role in these plans.
- To foster intelligence networks inland that should operate with independence of the counterrevolutionary organizations.
- To train and instruct agents, in the national territory, concerning guerrilla warfare, communications, intelligence, sabotage, and psywar.

The zones more used for infiltrations were:

In Oriente: Playitas, Guantánamo; Los Pozos, Yateras, southern coast; Caimanera; Baracoa, Guantánamo; Bahía de Báez, Nibujón, Baracoa, northern coast; Tres Piedras, border perimeter with the Naval Base of Guantánamo; Bahía de Navas, Baracoa, northern coast; Arroyo la Costa, Hatibonico, southern coast; Caletón Blanco Beach, southern coast; Boca de Dos Ríos, Barrio Aserradero, El Cobre.

In Camagüey: Laguna de la Leche.

In Las Villas: Canal Yurumao; El Guasí, Vueltas; Sierra Morena, north of Las Villas; Carahatas, north of Las Villas; Guajimico, southern coast of Las Villas; Punta Gorda, between Carahatas Beach and La Panchita, north of Las Villas.

In Matanzas: La Palma River, Cárdenas; Varadero.

In La Habana: Santa Cruz del Norte; Playa Baracoa; Bajos de Santa Ana, west Havana; Rosario, south Havana; Punta Roca, Santa Cruz del Norte.

In Pinar del Río: San Diego River, Los Palacios, Malas Aguas inlet, Puerto Esperanza, northern coast; Cabañas, Santa Lucía.[2]

PARAMILITARY TERRORIST OPERATIONS

Papers consulted in the MININT archives concerning paramilitary operations indicate that more than thirty actions of significant character —defined as attacks from planes and speed boats on economic targets in the coast line and cities aimed at sabotage and terrorism—were carried out in 1962.

Also, foreign ships involved in the Cuban trade were targets of these operations. These attacks were carried out against ships in Cuban ports or in international waters near the Cuban coasts.

The undertaking of attacks to boats of the Cuban Revolutionary Navy and Cuban fishing boats were also contemplated.

Some of the zones of the country subject to paramilitary operations were: in Oriente, through Cayo Mambí and Baracoa; in Camagüey, through Morón, Romano and Francés Cays; in Las Villas, through Cádiz Bay, Remedios, Trinidad, Cienfuegos, Caibarién, and Sagua la Grande; in Matanzas, through Matanzas Bay, and Cárdenas; in La Habana, through Surgidero de Batabanó, northern coast of Havana city, and Santa Cruz del Norte; in Pinar del Río, through Carraguao Point, Candelaria, Los Palacios, and Caleta de Humo.

The bombarding of areas in Havana city coastline on August 24, 1962, against the Sierra Maestra Hotel, the Chaplin Theater, and fellow-student residences in Miramar suburb are among the paramilitary operations to be mentioned. The action was carried out by two speed boats, furnished with artillery, coming from the United States.

Likewise, on September 10, 1962, a speed boat furnished with artillery, machine-gunned the Cuban boat *San Pascual* and the British ship *New Lane* in front of Francés Cay, in Sancti Spíritus, while loading sugar. And on October 8, 1962, a speed boat attacked port facilities in Isabela de Sagua, Las Villas. Both actions were undertaken by the terrorist organization Alpha 66, settled in the United States. In 1962, the CIA created Alpha 66 to carry out paramilitary operations against Cuba in the context of the Operation Mongoose.

---

2. This distribution was made according to the then political-administrative division of the country, by means of which Cuba was divided into six provinces. *Ed.*

In 1962 and according to information consulted in the MININT archives, the bodies of the State Security investigated more than fifty significant operational cases in which espionage was one of the main directions.

In this period it was seen that the enemy·agents, together with espionage activity, intervened in sabotage plans, terrorist actions, organizations of counterrevolutionary groups in rural areas, operational supply to counterrevolutionary organizations, infiltrations and exfiltrations, backing to psywar actions and involvement in plots of assassination of leaders of the Cuban Revolution, particularly, against the Commander in Chief.

Who were those men and women that the CIA recruited in this period and its modus operandi to execute its intelligence operations during the Operation Mongoose and Multi-track Program in 1963?

When examining the main espionage cases, we can point out the following characteristics that the recruited agents by the CIA in the period showed:
- They had had links with Batista's tyranny; had had responsibilities of political, military character, or had been public officials.
- They had belonged to traditional parties, which had had posts during Ramón Grau San Martín's and Carlos Prío Socarrás' administrations, in political, administrative activities, and in the armed institutions.
- They were professionals with broad relations with former representatives of the high industrial, sugar, landowning, and import-commercial bourgeoisie.
- They were Cuban émigrés settled in the United States that, in some cases, had fought in the ranks of the U.S. Armed Forces during the World War II.
- They were members of the Cuban bourgeois economic elite, whose interests were organically associated to the U.S. capital invested in Cuba.
- They were members of counterrevolutionary organizations that confronted the Revolution.
- An important recruiting reserve for the CIA, were the leaders of catholic associations, which, with the support of the high religious hierarchy, had created their own counterrevolutionary structures. The MRR, the MRP, the DRE, and the MDC were among some, just to mention a few.

- They were former combatants against Batista's dictatorship and had betrayed the Revolution.

A very rooted anti-Communism, fanatic and irrational, notably influenced on persons of limited political culture who had been the target of propaganda campaigns unleashed by the United States Government as result of the Cold War and the East-West conflict.

In these analyses, the involvement of U.S. citizens residing in Cuba, as well as the activity developed by diplomatic representatives from other countries in Cuba, cannot be discarded.

The CIA organized its agents in small and big networks. Tasks that agents of these espionage cases received, almost invariably referred to military, economic and political intelligence; also, in some cases, studies of areas to carry out rebellions, to determine points of infiltration, or to create maritime reception cells to introduce weapons, technical means and other operational supplies.

The communications means used were: personal link, P.O. Box in other countries, hideouts (container), radio-telegraphy, conventional telephones, diplomatic luggage of diverse embassies of allies to the United States, (conventional) cables, short-wave radio (operational songs, which were keys and messages), and international mail.

In the case of communications, the means used were: secret writing; radio-communication with AT-3 plant, RR-44 plant, RR-48-A plant, RS-1 plant, and double film (latent image) and micropoint.

In some cases, the heads of networks were in touch with the main counterrevolutionary organizations which operated in Cuba. In this sense, and according to CIA estimates of October 1962, it should be underlined that the penetration of the G-2 in counterrevolutionary structures in Cuba was significant to such a point that CIA analysts considered that the counterrevolution, in that period, had lost possibilities to become a threat for the stability of the revolutionary power.

Another line of activity of the networks aimed at working with terrorist groups in mountain areas, with the purpose to forge the unity of these groups with the counterrevolutionary organizations, and to put them under control of the CIA in a single counterrevolutionary front, what was to increase the vulnerabilities concerning confrontation possibilities in their task.

In many cases, the recruitment of agents for these networks was carried out through the offering of money, and it took place in the national territory, in the United States, or in third countries. The CIA JM-WAVE Station was in charge of the recruitment in the United States.

In some cases, this station used the Cuban Refugees Station at Opa Locka as a disguise.

The training program of recruited agents in the United States, for those with access to the U.S. territory, consisted in: secret writing, method to obtain intelligence, shooting practical classes, preparations for undertaking sabotage, and training in explosives C-3, C-4, and TNT.

The Section of Special Missions, to which the commands undertaking actions of paramilitary and terrorist character subordinated, operated in the JM-WAVE Station. Among its essential characteristics, it should be pointed out that:

- They were mainly recruited among counterrevolutionary émigrés, trained in the camps of Guatemala or Panama during preparations for the invasion of the Bay of Pigs in 1961.
- There were chosen, mainly, individuals, with good educational level and final preparation to carry out tasks as radiomen and frogmen.

The training of these commands, subordinated to the CIA Station JM-WAVE, comprised: explosives, demolition, weaponry, intelligence and counter-intelligence, methodology for terrorist actions, guerrilla warfare, specific training for command, specific training for frogmen, handling and use of rafts, driving and use of speed-boats, handling and use of phonics, invisible writing, survival, recognition and use of photographic cameras.

For communication and secret link with the CIA Station in the United States, the commands used sophisticated equipments such as RS-1 and RS-6 plants; communication through phonics was carried out with the equipments PRC-10, and PRC-6, and others of commercial manufacturing. Also, they trained in the use of infrared lights, white-light lanterns, flares, and light tracers.

The CIA was not only willing to undertake its actions through the counterrevolutionary organizations, but it also conceived the creation of intelligence networks. The most important case was the FUO, a network organized by Esteban Márquez (agent Plácido) in Pinar del Río Province. Former military men of the tyranny, relatives of counterrevolutionary prisoners made up its membership, and also citizens affected by revolutionary laws.

Esteban Márquez Novo upraised in Pinar del Río mountains in 1960, as a member of the counterrevolutionary organization Movement of Constitutional Recovery (MRC). When the military operation began against this movement, he took refuge at the Argentina embassy. Once he was abroad, the CIA in Venezuela recruited him. Márquez Novo, from bourgeois origin and frank anti-Communist and pro-American filiation, had worked at the Cuban-American Cultural Institute. In March 1962, he infiltrated through Pinar del Río coast. In the record of the State Security on the FUO it is stated the following:

> Esteban Márquez Novo's mission was to create an espionage network and recruit individuals sympathetic to the revolutionary cause for, in a certain moment—after having received enough military materiel—spread chaos and destruction in support to an invasion from outside of Cuba. While this plan was forged, the espionage network was to be in charge in obtaining all kind of possible political, military, and economic intelligence, which was to be transmitted to the United States through the RS-1 portable plants.
>
> In order to undertake his mission, he had to make contact with the remains of his former organization, the Movimiento de Resistencia Constitucional, and to do so, he went to his brother-in-law's house, Gerardo Rodríguez Arango. This house that he baptized as the Contact Position, was used for his stay during some months while restructuring his old organization and while making way to make some recruitments of higher importance.[3]

Márquez Novo organized the general staff of the network, created diverse working fronts called commands; the first three in Pinar del Río Province, other three in La Habana and one in the Isle of Pines (Isle of Youth at present). The network kept operating through the whole 1962; in 1963, he established two new commands: the one for communications and the other for instruction aimed at ground training for chosen members of the network. This latter was supplied with weapons, ammunitions, communication equipments, explosives, and war materiel in order to have an arsenal to supply the groups that were to be upraised in arms the "D-day" (the day of invasion of Cuba by the United States). His main task consisted in initially sending military intelligence to CIA headquarters. They were subsequently to undertake sabotage and to facilitate an uprising to support the U.S. invasion.

The FUO worked from 1962 to 1964 when the Cuban authorities neutralized it.

This big network had eight CIA agents, who received instruction in the United States during ten-month courses. The linking methods with

3. Record of the Western United Front (FUO). CIHSE Archives.

the station were through AT-3 and RS-1 plants, secret writing, infiltration/exfiltration maritime reception, which were used to make sketches and military drawings; personal contacts with the Chief of the network, skippers of fishing boats used as links in the high seas; conventional phrases in a program of Radio Americas broadcasting station.

The FUO disposed of nine positions for maritime receptions; three of these were used—and five for air receptions. Eight permanent hideouts and three temporary ones were used.

The FUO operation could not achieve the goals proposed by the CIA. The last messages sent by agent Plácido to the CIA station in the United States in 1964 are revealing; they prove the lack of capability of the network to confront challenges of organizing the uprising inside of Cuba, the lack of motivations and convictions to continue the struggle, the sense of feeling manipulated and abandoned by the CIA, and the recognition that they could not count on a base of popular support for implementing their plans.[4]

The FUO was conceived in the context of the Operation Mongoose as one of the most important subversive means in which the CIA had put its hopes to make the Revolution unstable.

In the operation of liquidation were seized: 207 automatic weapons, 2500 bullets, 46 guns, hundreds of hand-grenades, 256 bars of plastic explosives C-4, 1576 units which included small explosive devices, pencil-thin time bombs, 6 radio-automatic equipments used for communications with the JM-WAVE station and among them.[5]

The FUO was the biggest intelligence network ever organized by the U.S. intelligence services in their secret war on Cuba. Its subversive profile identified itself with Mongoose from the priority that military intelligence had and its purpose to create a clandestine army inside Cuba. It is possible to wonder if this was rather an operation of the U.S. military intelligence agencies.

When making a qualitative assessment on the quality of intelligence recollected by the CIA agents in the national territory, we can conclude that:

- Consulted papers allow deducing and stating that the CIA could not penetrate key sectors of the revolutionary institutions.

4. In the record of the FUO, at the CIHSE Archives, there are the messages the network sent to the station, what allows us to make this assertion.
5. Fabián Escalante Font, *La Guerra Secreta contra Cuba* [The Secret War on Cuba] (Havana: Editorial Capitán San Luis, 1993).

- The response of the bodies of the State Security allowed to neutralize important enemy actions, discover its plans and intentions, and to know the main intelligence requirements.
- The Central Intelligence Agency could not achieve, with its agents in Cuba, the intelligence requirements foreseen in the Operation Mongoose.

IRREGULAR WARFARE

Within the Operation Mongoose, the undertaking of irregular warfare was present since its beginning.

For Edward Landsdale, the organization of irregular groups in different provinces of Cuba aimed at creating conditions for spreading war to cities from the countryside, after forming an irregular army projected during the fifth phase of the Mongoose schedule, called Resistance. This fifth phase was to be executed between August and September 1962 as previous action of the sixth phase aimed at the overthrowing of the Revolution in October of that year.

For the CIA and the Pentagon, the creation of a national front of counterrevolutionary detachments in the mountains, whose general headquarters would be at the Escambray Mountains, was fundamental for establishing a strategic alliance and strategic collaboration with urban counterrevolutionary organizations; thus, a single bloc of the counterrevolutionary movement in Cuba was to be created, directed from the general headquarters of the Operation Mongoose in Washington, which would be in charge of starting the armed insurrection nationwide, a previous step to facilitate and support the decisive U.S. military intervention.

Between late May and early June 1961, and through the counterrevolutionary organizations, the enemy sent instructions to the heads of terrorist groups of the 120-150 elements who had survived in the Escambray Mountains after April 1961, in order to be reorganized for future plans to confront the Revolution. It is precisely in June 1961 when a process of new grouping of these terrorists—who kept hid in areas of difficult access in the Escambray, in the plains of Trinidad coast, south Sancti Spíritus, and in the borders of Camagüey Province—began to take place. In these actions, the main counterrevolutionary organizations in Cuba and the CIA agents of political actions intervened, under the orientation of the CIA headquarters to establish contacts with these groups.

In June 1961, an important CIA agent and other ringleaders of the counterrevolution organization MRR succeeded in contacting the head of the groups at the Escambray in order to coordinate the actions of these groups with the ones of the Front of Revolutionary Unity (FUR), whose headquarters was in Havana and was directed by three CIA agents.

Coincidentally, the MRR cells operating in Trinidad, Sancti Spíritus, Placetas, Cumanayagua, Santa Clara, Fomento, Caibarién and Cienfuegos tried to logistically support these bands.

In this context, it is important to note that after the defeat at the Bay of Pigs, the heads of the bands made efforts to achieve greater independence of the counterrevolutionary organizations, although not refusing financial and material assistance.

The groups began diverse terrorist actions in areas chosen to operate, such as the assassination of the literacy campaigner Manuel Ascunce Domenech and the campesino Pedro Lantigua Ortega on November 26, 1961.

From the moment President John F. Kennedy approved the Operation Mongoose on November 30, 1961, the revolutionary forces launched a new offensive against the counterrevolutionary bands.

According to social-historical research carried out between April 29 and December 26, 1961, eight infiltrations of "commands," associated to the creation of uprising focuses in different points of Cuba, took place.

A significant signal of the role assigned to irregular warfare in the Program Mongoose is evident in the instructions given from the JM-WAVE station to counterrevolutionary organizations, particularly, to the MRR and the MRP, in order to logistically support the bands and to coordinate their actions.

At the time, the Naval Base of Guantánamo developed an intense intelligence, subversive, terrorist, and operational supply activity to internal counterrevolution. The Naval Intelligence Service (NIS) of the U.S. Navy was the mechanism used to facilitate huge resources for the counterrevolutionary organizations. It also provided the infiltration of commands.

The sociological analysis of these groups reveal their inherent characteristics of the social scum, lacking ethical, political, and cultural patterns, without any strengthened principle in their individual-and-collective psychology. They feel motivated by instincts of hatred against the Revolution work and its symbols, by mercenary convictions; they are devoted to crime, terror, and receivers of anti-Communist propaganda campaigns, with a low educational level. Being inheritors of the tyranny's henchmen, they are an easy instrument for plans and intentions of the enemy. Organically linked in almost all cases to landowners, whose properties were nationalized by the Agrarian Reform of 1961, they were obedient and submissive to the orders of their national masters and, for extension, of the empire that exerted control over them.

What was always the intention of the "guerrilla army of Mongoose"? To wait for the United States invasion; to evade the frontal fight on the revolutionary forces; to carry out terrorist and sabotage actions on farming production; to assassinate campesinos, agricultural workers and their families; to spread panic and terror to support the plans of counterrevolutionary armed insurrection from rural areas of the country without exposing to combat against the Rebel Army and the militias.

In the early days of January 1962, a CIA agent infiltrated through Santa Cruz del Norte in La Habana Province. Amongst his tasks it was that of coordinating, with heads of the bands in Matanzas Province, the recruitment of individuals that might be trained in the United States for the guerrilla warfare.

In February 1962, and from the Naval Base at Guantánamo, two CIA commands landed through Playitas, Baracoa, in order to create a network aimed at fostering uprisings in the region. After fulfilling this task and burning different schools, they run away to the Base.

In April and from the Naval Base at Guantánamo, two CIA agents infiltrated with the mission to open different focuses. This action was frustrated. By late April, and using the same way, other two CIA agents infiltrated through the area of Lajas, Guantánamo, with identical purposes; they also were subsequently arrested.

By early May 1962, the CIA dropped an agent in parachutes, in the vicinity area of Navas, northern coast of Baracoa, who should remain in the region for two months in order to study the area for three main goals to fulfill: weapon droppings, future landings, and creation of terrorist groups. A month later, in June, the CIA agent was arrested during a military operation unleashed by the revolutionary forces.

In June 1962, an infiltration team penetrated through Arroyo la Costa beach, with the mission to create terrorist groups in the mountains of Oriente Province. The mission of this CIA operation, which extended from June to December 1962, consisted in the recollection of intelligence, and to create focuses in Baracoa, Gran Piedra, and Chivirico. Also it included the spread of operational areas to the borders of Oriente and Camagüey provinces, and to coordinate the activity between Oriente and Las Villas. These plans were neutralized in January 1963.

If one of the main directions of the JM-WAVE Station was aimed at creating counterrevolutionary focuses, supporting armed groups in the mountains of the six existing provinces in Cuba at the time, and forging an alliance of the counterrevolutionary organizations with these groups, without skimping means or resources, the Revolution could grasp, from the very beginning, the dimension and significance of the enemy plans and intentions.

From mid 1961, the Revolutionary Armed Forces and the bodies of the State Security reinforced the fighting against the bands, which entered into an increased phase on July 3, 1962. The Chief of the Central Army of the country, Commander Juan Almeida Bosque, signed an order constituting the Section of Fight against Bandits in Las Villas and Camagüey. Subsequently, and during the whole August, the order was put into practice in the rest of the provinces.

Confrontation methods were improved, and the fight against groups became more efficient from a better use of human and technical resources, an adequate distribution of forces, and a greater coordination between troops in operation, the bodies of the State Security and political and mass organizations.

In 1962, the activity of these groups covered all provinces of the country, for a total of 118 groups with 1580 members.

The main scenario in which the struggle against bandits took place was the Escambray Mountains, region chosen by the CIA from the beginning to spread its mechanism of irregular warfare against the Revolution. The causes that determined the use of this territory are well identified and established, and they are in correspondence with evident studies and intelligence assessments undertaken by the analysts of the Agency. In terms of the geography of the area, the Escambray Mountains are located in the middle-south of Cuba, in the bridge-province between western and eastern provinces.

Trinidad city was a territory with certain enemy potential that was willing to collaborate and to facilitate subversive activity in the mountains, with the additional advantage of having an airport and a seaport, Casilda, which allowed the undertaking of air and sea operations in perspective.

The social-and-demographic characteristics of the Escambray were determined by a specific structure of the land property: the campesino population was mainly made up of small farmers. With a population of about 630,000 inhabitants, approximately 260,000 of these lived in rural areas, what reflects the social-and-operational importance of the region.

According to statistics, when the Revolution triumphed, there were 31,073 illiterate people; for December 1961, 23,730 people had already been taught to read and write.

During the insurrectional fight at the Escambray, the Directorate of the Second National Front of the Escambray was the responsible for vandalic and assassination acts. This had created, amongst some residents in those regions, a distorted image of the revolutionary combatants in the territory seized by this organization. Its main leaders boycotted the activities that the troops of the Revolutionary Movement March 13, Revolutionary Movement July 26, and the Popular Socialist Party developed.

The topography facilitated the execution of the irregular warfare, with difficult ways of access to the mountainous range for troops in operations. Despite these objectives characteristics for irregular warfare, the terrorists could not fulfilled the Mongoose goals of fighting a war in the mountains in spite of the resources that the enemy succeeded in giving.

As a result of their terrorist actions, seventy-seven people were killed and other twenty-seven wounded. the victims of these actions are distributed according to the following categories: one boy, forty campesinos, fourteen militiamen, six workers of different sectors, five laborers, three school-teachers, two leaders of the National Association of Small Farmers (ANAP), three combatants of the MININT, one administrator of a farm, one free-lance worker, and one leader of the Integrated Revolutionary Organizations (ORI). Wounded people were concentrated in nineteen campesinos, four militiamen, one boy, one leader of the ORI, one agricultural worker, and one student.

Assassinations concentrated in Las Villas (thirty), Matanzas (eleven), and La Habana (eight), while in Pinar del Río and Oriente two people were killed and in Camagüey one person was killed.

The counterrevolutionary violence was confronted by the revolutionary forces: the Rebel Army, the Ministry of the Interior, the Revolutionary National Militias, and the battalions of the Fight against Bandits, which defeated the CIA plans aimed at turning the Escambray into a bulwark of the counterrevolution in the mountains.

The counterrevolutionary bands never seized an area or established in a determined territory, and they never went beyond nomadic phase of guerrilla activity.

PLANS OF ASSASSINATIONS AFTER THE DEFEAT OF BAY OF PIGS

A general analysis of the subversive activity after the Bay of Pigs permits revealing that the assassination of the Commander in Chief and other main leaders of the Revolution was one of the main strategic directions of plans on Cuba, associated in the most important cases to the creation of conditions which would facilitate the direct military intervention of the United States Government.

Why did the CIA opt to immediately adapt these plans? Why was the operational situation not deeply assessed, having in mind that the Taylor Commission was evaluating the causes and conditions, which determined the failure of the Bay of Pigs, whose judgment was to be issued in June 1961? Was the CIA in conditions to undertake its ambitious projects of executive actions, despite the setback experienced by the internal counterrevolution in April 1961 when the headquarters of its fifth-column had been under arrest, or was running away from the revolutionary justice?

How could the CIA recover its credibility before the Kennedy administration?

The CIA specialists agreed that it was indispensable to immediately unleash plots to assassinate the top leader of the Revolution, while Fidel headed the political vanguard of the first socialist revolution in the Western Hemisphere.

Using its agents in Cuba, who had not been discovered by the State Security during the days of the Bay of Pigs, and using the counterrevolutionary organizations inside and outside of Cuba were the safest ways to guarantee the principle of the plausible denial, allowing disguise the truly CIA purposes.

The main activities related with the plots to assassinate the top Cuban leadership were controlled, tracked, and conceived by agents of the U.S. intelligence agencies who were operating inside the counterrevolutionary structures in the national territory and outside of Cuba, and which were fulfilling these tasks according to indications of the United States Government.

In the period between the first quarter of 1961 to November 1962 there is no evidence of significant plan of attempt to crime in which a CIA agent is not present as an important element of the counterrevolutionary organization that prepared, conceived, and planned the action. In all these plans the anonymous, devoted, clandestine and sacred labor of revolutionary men and women, who in due time discovered, or identified the purposes of these actions, were present.

No counterrevolutionary organization operated independently of the CIA, or other inteligence agencies in the development of these plans. There was always present a link of the operational chain of these agencies.

Never in this history, the U.S. intelligence agencies have publicly recognized their determinant involvement in these plans, with the exception of the ones exposed in the declassified paper: *Reports on plots to assassinate Fidel Castro,* elaborated by the Inspector General of the Central Intelligence Agency Jack Earman, in March and April 1967 according to indication of Richard Helms, Director of the CIA, and delivered to him on April 24, 1967.

In the memorandum of this report it is pointed out that:

This reconstruction of agency involvement in plans to assassinate Fidel Castro is at best an imperfect history. Because of the extreme sensitivity of the operations being discussed or attempted as a matter of principle no official records where kept of planning, of approvals, or of implementation. The few written records that do exist are either largely tangential to the main events or put on paper from memory years afterwards.[6]

The release of the report made by the Inspector General of the CIA in 1967 implies a paradox: it hides the truly dimension, magnitude, and significance of the executive actions that does not know geographic borders and does not recognize all the principles of political ethics that should characterize relations between the states based on the International Law.

The paper recognizes that:

It became clear very early in our investigation that the vigor with which schemes where pursued within the Agency to eliminate Castro personally varied with the intensity of the U.S. Government's efforts to overflow the Castro regime. We can identify five separated faces in Agency assassination planning, although the transitions from one to another are not always sharply defined. Each face is a re-

---

6. Editors at Prevailing Winds Research, *CIA Assassination Plots. A Report from the Inspector General on Plots to Assassinate Fidel Castro.* Introduction by Peter Dale Scott, Ph.D., August 4, 1994.

flection of the them [*sic*] prevailing Government attitude toward the Cuban regime.[7]

Following the evolution of plans of attempted murders was established, only admitted by the United States Government as responsibility of its intelligence agencies.

The first phase comprised prior August 1960. In the report, there is pointed out that the projects identified prior of about August 1960, except one, were apparently bound for trying to discredit the Commander in Chief, influencing on his behavior, or modifying his appearance.

Concerning the period between August 1960 and April 1961, it is pointed out that conspiracies were conceived in aggressive way, and considered, at least by one of its planners, just as a matter of a whole general pledge for overthrowing the regime, which ended in the Bay of Pigs.

The period between April 1961 (after the Bay of Pigs) to late 1961 (early Mongoose) belongs to the third phase, in which according to the report, a principal project (plan) that started in August 1960 was canceled after the Bay of Pigs and remained paralyzed for some months.

From late 1961 to late 1962, fourth phase, a specific project was reactivated in early 1962, and once again, was vigorously in progress in the times of Mongoose, within a climate of intense pressure on the part of the administration concerning the CIA, in order to carry out something on Castro and his Cuba.

The fifth phase corresponds to the period post-Missile Crisis and the collapse of Mongoose. Here it is indicated that an aggressive project, which began in August 1960 and was reactivated in April 1962, finally concluded in early 1963.

Two plans, born in 1963, had no possible feasibility, and nothing concerning this was done.

The only concrete facts of plans for attempted murders that the CIA recognizes, during its forty-two years of aggressions on Cuba as the only ones where it was involved, were the following:

Attempts of assassination between March and August 1960

1. Use of chemical substances for contamination in the radio station where Fidel Castro made his interventions. This was not approved due to lack of feasibility.

---

7. Id.

2. Preparation of contaminated tobacco for delivering to Fidel and provoking a temporary disturbance in his behavior during a public intervention. It was not executed because the CIA did not have secure possibilities of access.

3. Plan to make Fidel lost his beard and thus destroy his public image, even though an excessive use of the product could provoke paralysis. The project did not progress.

4. Plans of CIA-Mob to provoke the physical elimination of the Commander in Chief.

August 1960

The CIA coordinated with elements of the U.S. Gambling Syndicate, which were operating in Havana, to organize a plot to assassinate Fidel Castro. In September, the CIA and the Mob made contacts. During the third and fourth quarters of the year the possible methods to be used were examined. On August 16, 1960 the Technical Operation Division received a box of cigars to be prepared with lethal substances. The cigars were to produce immediate death. The cigars were stored and destroyed in 1963.

January-February 1961

The CIA-Mob conspiracy continued. This time they proposed to use small pills of the size of saccharin tablets. A substance known as botulin was chosen. It was assumed that the Mob had ways to deliver the pills to the Commander in Chief. The Chairman of the Executive Actions Unit ZR-Rifle William K. Harvey, followed the operation as representative of the Chief for the CIA Clandestine Services Richard Bissell.

Late February-March 1961

Elements of the Mob introduced the pills in Cuba, these were delivered to a contact of the Mob, who should carry out the operation, but this contact retreated from the game.

March-April 1961

The Mob informed the CIA that was in contact with a leader of the counterrevolutionary emigration who might help and be involved in the plan of attempt to assassination. This person accepted the proposal of the Mob, which delivered the pills to be introduced in Cuba.

April-May 1961

The CIA, after the Bay of Pigs, informed the Mob that the Operation was canceled.

Late 1961-Early 1962 (Mongoose)

Once again, William K. Harvey assumed the operation of the plan of assassination of Castro, with the Mob collaboration. In his present condition as Chairman of the Cuban Task Force of the CIA, in the Program Mongoose, and in the Executive Actions Unit ZR-Rifle, he placed the plan of attempts on Fidel Castro's life amongst the main directions of ZR-Rifle.

April 1962

William K. Harvey met with representatives of the Mob to coordinate actions concerning the undertaking of the plan of attempt of assassination, which an agent would carry out in a restaurant often visited by Fidel Castro. The agent would poison the food of the top leader of the Revolution.

The leader of the counterrevolutionary emigration was in touch with the Mob. It was he the one who had contact in Havana to carry out the plan.

The counterrevolutionary ringleader received the pills (one capsule and three pills) for the attempt of assassination—from the Mob through the CIA—and requested weapons and equipments from the Mob to support the Operation. The CIA, through the JM-WAVE, delivered explosives, detonators, twenty rifles caliber-30, twenty guns caliber-45, two radios, and a speed-boat with radar for the attempted murder.

May 1962

The pills were in the hands of the contact of the counterrevolutionary ringleader who worked in the restaurant where the Commander in Chief usually went.

June 1962

The Mob representative reported William K. Harvey that the contact in the counterrevolutionary emigration had sent an infiltration team made up of three men, just in case the opportunity for the assassination was possible, or to recruit individuals to carry out the operation, maybe using the pills. Harvey never knew their names or other data.

September 1962

The pills were in a safe place, so was the infiltration team.

Plans of attempts to crime in early 1963

5. Preparing a diving suit in which a fungus—provoking a skin disease of chronic character that will contaminate the respiratory system

with tuberculosis bacillus—would spread. This plan was given up for a lack of feasibility.

6. A marine shell prepared with explosives was to be placed in an area where Fidel Castro dived. The shell should attract his attention so when taking it an explosion would occur. A mini-submarine was to be used to put it. This was considered not to be feasible.

7. Am-Lash Project (1961-1966). The former Commander of the Rebel Army, traitor to the Revolution and CIA agent, Rolando Cubela Secades, was to be used to carry out, together with other counterrevolutionary elements, an attempt on the Commander in Chief's life. The CIA associated this plan with the need to start an internal rebellion to allow and determine the United States support, probably sponsored by the OAS.

The analyses elaborated by the bodies of the MININT in the period post-Bay of Pigs towards early Operation Mongoose, in November 1961, describe and explain other operations of the United States intelligence agencies concerning plots to assassinate the Commander in Chief.

The Central Intelligence Agency, after the Bay of Pigs, guided one of its main agents in Cuba the undertaking of attempts on the Commander in Chief's life, and against the Minister of the Revolutionary Armed Forces, Commander Raúl Castro that should be undertaken on July 26, 1961. The CIA coordinated this operation with the Naval Intelligence Service of the Naval Base of Guantánamo.

The agent had traveled to the United States in May 1961, and had interviewed with the Advisor of President Kennedy for Counter-Insurgency Affairs, member of the United States National Security Council and Chairman of the Presidential Commission, General Taylor, who investigated the causes and conditions of the Bay of Pigs failure. He was also one of the intellectual authors of the Operation Mongoose.

The plan comprised the following actions:
- Attempting on the Commander Raúl Castro's life during the rally to be held at the stadium in Santiago de Cuba, on the occasion of July 26.
- In case this action failed, another aggression was to be carried out when the Commander Raúl went for the airport, in the intersection of El Morro and the airport roads.
- A counterrevolutionary command, ambushed in a farm near the Naval Base of Guantánamo, in which they were hidden, would fire seven mortars on the Base and on a unit of the Rebel Army, near this Base, simulating an aggression from Cuba in response

to the attempt on the Commander Raúl's life. This situation was to be the ideal pretext for the United States military intervention in Cuba.
- Simultaneously, a plan of attempt on the Commander in Chief's life was to be executed during a rally at the Revolution Plaza, in Havana, in association with sabotage executed in Santiago de Cuba, Las Villas, and Camagüey.

According to research undertaken, a new attempt of assassination started to be forged on June 4, 1961, during a meeting between a CIA emissary, other from the FRD with different counterrevolutionary ringleaders. The plotted elements had close links with the Naval Intelligence Service of the Naval Base of Guantánamo, which facilitated all means for undertaking this action. Some sabotages against ships anchored at Havana port were associated to the attempted murder. The means for its execution came from the Naval Base of Guantánamo.

The counterrevolutionary organizations M-30-11, MRP, and FRD were to carry out another plan of attempt of assassination in July 1961, following orientations of the CIA agents. The plotters were in contact with officials of the Naval Intelligence Service of the Naval Base of Guantánamo.

In the last quarter of 1961, the Central Intelligence Agency, through one of its agents in the MRP planned another attempt on the Commander in Chief and other Revolution leaders' lives to be executed at the Presidential Palace, on the occasion of the President of the Republic's return, Osvaldo Dorticós, from a travel to Socialist countries. This terrorist action was to be preceded by some sabotages in different department stores in Downtown Havana. All these plans were conveniently neutralized.

So far, the first cases of attempt of assassination discovered and frustrated by the State Security in the period post-Bay of Pigs up to the arrival of the Operation Mongoose, in November 1961, which also was to be characterized by the preparations of other plans of attempts of assassination, already known some of them, as it was mentioned, in the released governmental papers.

From 1961, the Executive Actions Unit ZR-Rifle, headed by William K. Harvey, had been created to develop operations of political assassination of leaders considered enemies or hostile to the interests of the United States National Security Council. With the establishment of the Program Mongoose, Harvey was also to assume the responsibility of Chairman of the CIA Cuban Task Force, in charge of conducting oper tions, which were launched on Cuba from the JM-WAVE Station.

CHAPTER V. The Final Outcome

THE OPERATION MONGOOSE IN THE CUBAN ARENA.
A BAY OF PIGS IN SECRET

In 1962, The United States already considered the economic blockade on Cuba as *conditione sine qua non* of its subversive and unbalancing strategy. According to the U.S. Government, it was creating the necessary objective conditions for unchaining the counterrevolution. That is, the basic premise of Mongoose was to create domestic conditions by the use of foreign measures to provoke adverse social and political processes in the Cuban society leading to an inside uprising in the context of military invasion plans. Cuba was accused of subverting the dictatorships in Latin America when, in fact, it was the United States the one that had exported counterrevolution, counterinsurgency, neo-capitalist reforms, and peace corps. The Alliance for Progress was its best evidence; the Kennedy Panamericanism was its clearest ideological expression.

In January 1962, during the 8th Consultation Meeting of the Organization of American States the expulsion of Cuba from that organization was agreed. The suspension of every trade and weapon sale from any Latin American country was requested in the final resolution. Brazil, Argentina, Mexico, Chile, Ecuador and Bolivia abstained. Cuba therefore could not participate in Inter-American Defense Board activities, although in practice, the Revolutionary Government was never involved in them. It is good not to forget that in Cuba was a United States military mission, providing advisory to Fulgencio Batista's army in its struggle on the Rebel Army. As soon as the Revolution took power, the Revolutionary Government decided the suspension of this advisory and the departure of the American mission.

On February 3, 1962, President Kennedy signed the Presidential Proclamation 3447 in which it was established the complete blockade in the trade between Cuba and the United States; its implementation was to correspond to the Departments of Treasure and Commerce.

It was not a mere chance that the 8th Consultation Meeting of the OAS was held in January 1962. For that date, the Project of the Program Mongoose—the most complex system of subversive activity that the United States mounted in the post-war—was elaborated.

Cuba remained steady, calm, decided and daring. The 2nd Declaration of Havana constituted the description and explanation of Cuba policy in relation to the United States and the Latin American policy of the Revolution. Its central core was: "the duty of every revolutionary man is to make the Revolution." From then on, Cuba was a Latin American country, judicially isolated from the inter-American system, but constituted the political, ideological, and theoretical vanguard of the revolutionary movement in Latin America and the Caribbean.

On April 10, 1962, President Kennedy met with the Chairman of the Cuban Revolutionary Council, José Miró Cardona, in order to inform him on the policy adopted by the United States Government concerning Cuba. Miró told the following testimony of his meeting with Kennedy:

> The conference was lively and he [President Kennedy] assured me that the problem is essentially military and requiring six divisions [Miró Cardona intended this as a direct quote from Kennedy], that the Council should contribute the major contingent of soldiers and that we should not adopt a unilateral position because this would cause grave criticism in the continent. . . .
>
> He ended the conversation with words I can never forget. "Your destiny is to suffer. Do not weaken. You have my support and I reiterate my early pronouncements. Give the Council my most cordial regards."
>
> I left the White House with the assurance that the liberation of Cuba would follow soon with Cubans at the vanguard in battle.[1]

1. *New York Times,* April 19, 1962. Cited from Robert Scheer and Maurice Zeitlin, *Cuba: An American Tragedy*. (Great Britain: Penguin Books, 1964).

The year 1962 was difficult for the Cuban economy. The effects of one of the strongest dry seasons in the Cuban history were added to the tight measures of the blockade. Also, the consequences of changes in the extensive cultivation of sugar cane, using intensive methods and a policy of agricultural diversification, were undergone. The lack of technical equipments and chemical products to intensify cultivation was determined by the United States blockade. The enemy encouraged emigration of technicians and specialists in order to damage economy and social policy of the Revolution as much as possible. The 1962 sugar harvest was below expectations and Cuba could not fulfill its duties in the international market.

However, the enthusiasm of the people increased and the vast majority of the population backed the Revolution. During two years in power, the Revolution had made achievements that no other Latin American country could show. If the Bay of Pigs was a military prowess, in 1962 the Cuban society reflected truly social deed, fruit of a whole people in revolution. Let us see some examples:

- The Revolution established free medical assistance;
- Price of medicaments was reduced;
- Electric and gas tariffs were reduced;
- A recreation system was established, with reasonable prices, for the whole population;
- The Agrarian Reform Act was approved, turning sharecroppers and tenants into owners of the land;
- The free education was implemented for all educational levels (elementary, junior high, high school, and university);
- Unemployment, which had been a chronic problem in the Cuban society, was eliminated. It is important to remember that according to statistics, before 1959 unemployment in Cuba covered the 25% of the working force of the country;
- The Act to reduce rents for housing was approved;
- Illiteracy was eliminated in Cuba as result of the Literacy Campaign that never stopped in its mission of teaching to read and write the 100% of the illiterate population of the country. The 25% of the adult population were (approximately) illiterate in 1959;
- The education system for workers strengthened: continuation (third grade); improving courses for workers (sixth grade); and courses for minimum technical level. A total of 72,000 industrial workers, and 26,000 workers were registered in improving courses for minimum technical level.

In less than three years, the Revolution had provided labor security, social and economic advantages, which showed the existence of a government that defended independence, national sovereignty, and interests of the overwhelming majority of the population.

The political organization of the Cuban society was in frank process of strengthening. Young cadres, led by young leaders, quickly assimilated techniques and experiences that were to allow permanent and continuous progress of the Revolution through the path of Socialism.

The struggle against tyranny and imperialism had become the best forge to form revolutionaries. In order to protect sovereignty, territorial integrity, Socialism, fatherland, and the Revolution, the Cuban nation had forged an effective system of defense, assured by the Revolutionary Armed Forces and the Ministry of the Interior, with the essential and vital involvement of the people, armed and organized in the National Revolutionary Militias and the Committees for the Defense of the Revolution. The motto: Study, Work and Defense were not the expression of a propaganda slogan; it enclosed the political program of Cuban Socialism.

And to all this it must be added expressions of solidarity from the Socialist countries, of the USSR, of Eastern Europe and of the Popular Republic of China, in economic, military, technical assistance and credit grants terms. For Socialism on an international scale, Cuba represented not only the first Socialist revolution in the Western Hemisphere, but also the perspective to modify the correlation of forces between Socialism and Capitalism in the '60s. And also Cuba became in the paradigm of the Third World countries; it was the revolutionary choice, which came true.

THE DECLINE OF MONGOOSE

After the Cuban Missile Crisis of 1962, the Kennedy administration reviewed its subversive strategy on Cuba and determined the official suspension of the Program Mongoose in late November 1962. The crisis had introduced a new element in the scenario of the United States-USSR relations, USSR-Cuba relations and the historic United States-Cuba conflict.[2]

2. A complete, interesting, and valuable study on the significance of the Cuban Missile Crisis, was approached in the meeting of American, Soviet, and Cuban academicians, politicians, and scholars, held in Havana in 1992, where the Commander in Chief, Fidel Castro Ruz, was the main presenter on the Cuban part.

The Cuban stance had been clearly exposed in the Five Points enunciated by the Commander in Chief:

1. Cessation of the economic blockade;
2. Cessation of all subversive activities;
3. Cessation of terrorist attacks;
4. Cessation of all violations of our air-and-sea space;
5. Withdrawal of the Naval Base of Guantánamo.

(Deadline: October 29, 1962.)

In fact, already prior the emerging of the Cuban Missile Crisis, Mongoose was a defeated project. Our people dismantled the main CIA intelligence and subversive actions. The counterrevolutionary organizations were near death in October 1962, after the overwhelming strikes received between January and September 1962; the program of sabotage of the CIA Special Missions Group had been neutralized; irregular warfare was not a serious challenge for the Revolution stability any longer; plans of attempts on Commander in Chief's life were conveniently discovered and eliminated. The direct military invasion was the only alternative left, and in Mongoose plans this could only be unchained if previously an internal uprising have taken place in Cuba, whose perspectives were null in that period.

Mongoose meant the decline of the Gods, which Kennedy had chosen, to avenge the defeat of the Assault Brigade 2506 in Bay of Pigs and to destroy the Cuban Revolution, the second political setback of the Kennedy administration in its plans on Cuba.

APPENDIX

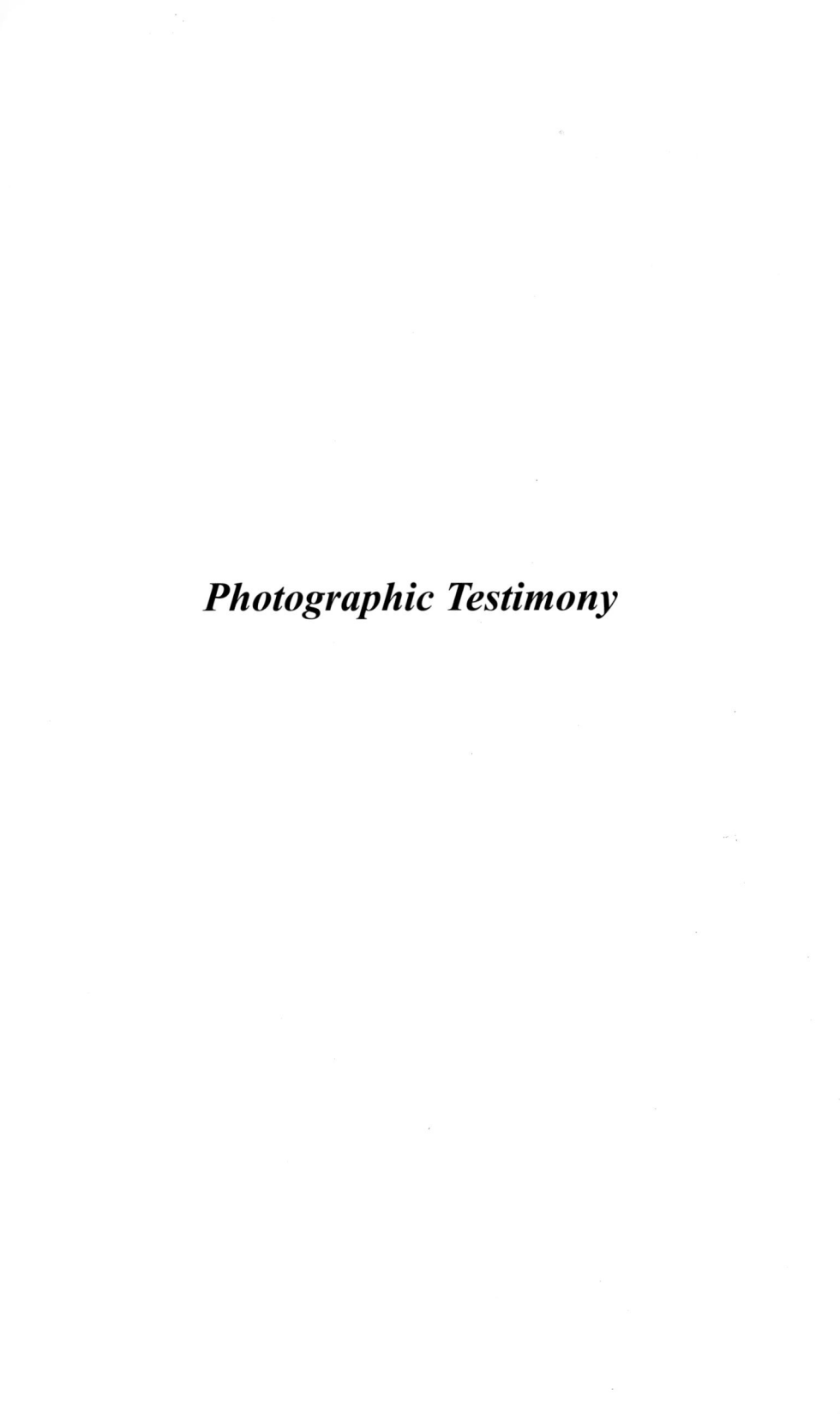

Photographic Testimony

The Naval Base of Guantánamo was largely used during the Operation Mongoose by the Naval Intelligence Service to foster espionage, terrorism, to support the creation of bandit groups in the mountains of Oriente, and to guarantee the supplying of means and resources to the internal counterrevolution.

General Edward Landsdale. Expert in counter-insurgency war with experience in Asian countries. The President John F. Kennedy appointed him as Chief of Operations, Operation Mongoose. His aureole of brilliant military strategist did not correspond with the evolution of Mongoose, which culminated in a deep failure.

Piracy attacks. One of the main directions of the Operation Mongoose consisted in carrying out pirate attacks on Cuban and foreign ships in trade with Cuba. This was an expression of the economic war, described in the plans of Mongoose. Fishing boats were frequent targets of sea pirates, as well as fishing areas.

Headquarters of the JM/WAVE Station in Florida, installed in 1962 at the Richmond air-naval station, in the outskirts of south Miami. Here, the Zenith Technical Enterprise Inc. was established, which was to be used as a façade by the CIA to justify its presence in this place.

John F. Kennedy, John McCone and Allan Dulles. In September 1961, President Kennedy made the decision to replace Allan Dulles as Director of the CIA: The myth of his invulnerability in the sands of the Bay of Pigs had vanished. The Kennedy administration put its hopes on McCone to guarantee its objective to overthrow the Cuban revolutionary power that confronted and defeated the complex covert operations unchained against the Island.

The CIA delivered its agents in Cuba the most modern communication means for the headquarters-agent and agent-headquarters contacts.

Fight against bandits. The Revolutionary Armed Forces, the Ministry of the Interior, and the Revolutionary National Militias destroyed CIA plans aimed at organizing counterrevolutionary groups upraised in the mountains to be used as a fifth-column, whose purposes were backing a military aggression from outside. The history of the counterrevolution in rural areas of the country is associated to crimes against the campesinos, sabotage to farming production, fires in rural schools and town's stores. The bands could never seize a town, or to go beyond the nomadic phase of the irregular warfare.

General Maxwell Taylor. Chief of the Board of the Joint Chief of Staff of the United States Armed Forces in 1962. In 1961, he chaired the commission that studied the causes and conditions of the failure the CIA had at the Bay of Pigs. He was the military chief who proposed kinds of special operations, which contributed to set the bases and principles of Operation Mongoose.

Richard Helms. In early 1962, he was appointed Under-director of Plans of the CIA (covert operations), replacing Richard Bissell, who had fallen in disgrace with the White House after the failure of the Bay of Pigs for having been the main responsible of the Operation Pluto. Helms took the Operation Mongoose as the CIA top priority in the period. He directly informed the Director of the CIA John McCone about the results of actions on Cuba. Helms' luck was not better that Bissell's. Mongoose was defeated despite refined strategies and subversion tactics, terrorism and intelligence implemented.

For the planning and organization of plans of attempts on Cuban leaders' lives, the CIA asked the Mafia to collaborate in these plans, in association with leaders of the counterrevolutionary organizations. One of these mobsters, linked with the ZR-Rifle, was Johnny Roselli.

One of the targets of sabotage plans of Mongoose was aimed at destroying the sugar industry. As an example, it is enough to point out that in 1962, more than 4000 counterrevolutionary actions in the sugar cane sector took place.

Ted Shackley. Chief of the JM-WAVE Station, considered as a truly clandestine empire of the CIA. The activities of this station are closely linked with the most tenebrous and sinister covert operations of the CIA on Cuba. Despite the huge technical, financial, and human resources at his disposal, and the unlimited backing of Langley, Shackley could not fulfill the entrusted tasks to subvert the Cuban Revolution.

William K. Harvey. He was the Chief of the Cuban Task Force in the general headquarter of the CIA in Langley, Virginia, during the development of the Operation Mongoose. Not by mere chance he was the Chief of the Program ZR-Rifle, aimed at carrying out actions of physical annihilation of foreign political leaders, considered hostile enemies to the United States national security interests. He was, also, in charge of directing and controlling activities at the CIA headquarters (JM-WAVE) in Florida, from which the operations of the Agency on Cuba, during the development of Mongoose, were carried out.

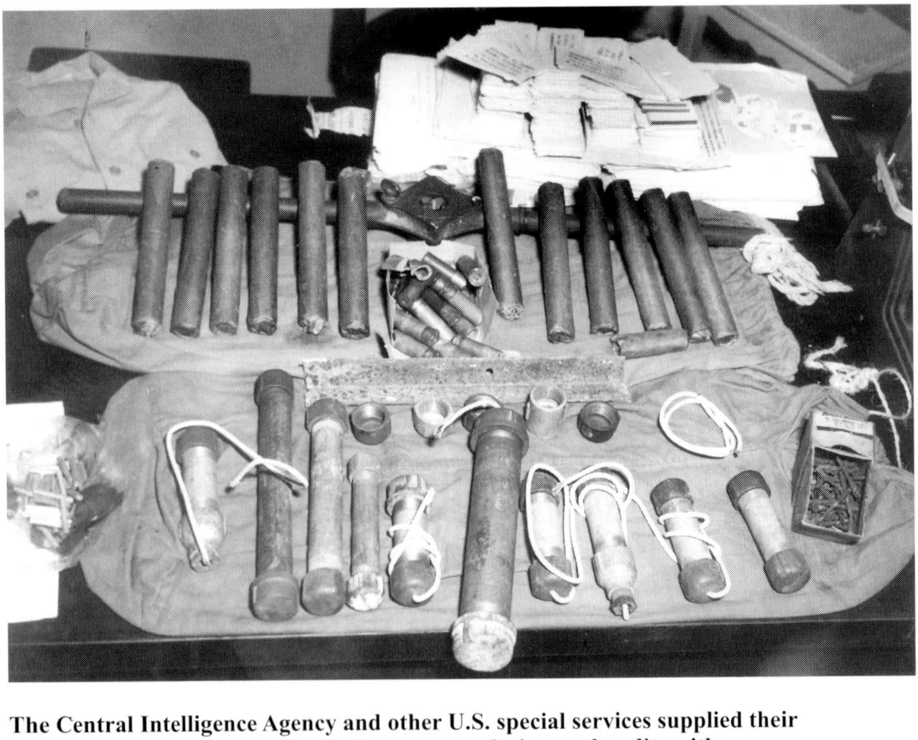

The Central Intelligence Agency and other U.S. special services supplied their agents, organizations and bands of counterrevolutionary bandits with weapons, ammunitions, and explosives. Maritime infiltrations were used, although air-droppings were also carried out; the latter, however, were fewer and more vulnerable to be captured.

Havana, June 21, 1962
Year of the Planning

To: Chief of the State Security Department
From: Chief of Section Q
Subject: IMPERIALIST PLANS ON THE CUBAN REVOLUTION[1]

A.- Plans of the Yankee[2] Central Intelligence Agency to be executed by
the so-called organization Revolutionary Recovery Movement, im-
mobilized with the arrest of its main leaders.
  a.- Main Plan.- JUAN MANUEL GUILLOT CASTELLANOS
  (agent) ROGELIO, agent of the Central Intelligence Agency
  and National Military Coordinator of the MRR (under arrest) is
  the main element, until the moment of his arrest, in charge, by
  CIA, to develop the plan that follows in details. In order to point
  out the counterrevolutionary influence and personality of this
  subject, we will tell that, despite of having less hierarchy than
  the National General Coordinator of the MRR (JUAN FALCÓN
  ZANMAR, under arrest), in practice he had major command-
  ing power and control of the organization than the above mentioned General Coordinator.
  The plan to be followed was:
  1.- Achieve unity of the estimated five organizations of national
    character, that is: PEOPLE'S REVOLUTIONARY
    MOVEMENT, CHRISTIAN DEMOCRATIC MOVE-
    MENT, STUDENT REVOLUTIONARY DIRECTOR-
    ATE, REVOLUTIONARY MOVEMENT NOVEM-
    BER 30 "FRANK PAIS," and the REVOLUTIONARY
    RECOVERY MOVEMENT. Unity referred to military mat-
    ter. Civilian aspect had not been taken into consideration
    yet.
    Unity was to be achieved at province level, appointing one
    of the five coordinators as Province Military Chief, to be

---

1. Excerpt of the original paper of the Ministry of the Interior.
2. For the majority in the United States this word means "a native or an inhabitant of
  the northern United States," but we, in Cuba, consider Yankee any citizen of that
  country. *Ed.*

trained abroad before starting to work, together a man of confidence of every unit to be trained in radiotelegraphy. During the period of training (three months) U.S. telegraphers were to come temporarily.

JUAN MANUEL GUILLOT CASTELLANOS alias ROGELIO held interviews with National Coordinators of the DRE and the MRP. The latter was in talks with the National Coordinators of the MDC and the MR-30-11. DEMOCRATIC REVOLUTIONARY RESCUE, and REVOLUTIONARY UNITY was initially included in the pact of unity, and JUAN MANUEL GUILLOT opposed them for considering these two last as "pocket organizations."

The CIA instructed JUAN MANUEL GUILLOT CASTELLANOS to personally interview with the National Coordinators of the MDC and the MR-30-11. If any satisfactory agreement was achieved concerning military effectiveness, they would give the necessary material for the plan of action that we detail as follows. GUILLOT CASTELLANOS held a previous interview with these coordinators, being summoned for Sunday of that week in Varadero Beach. Saturday night the National Coordinator of the DRE was arrested and a few days after JUAN MANUEL GUILLOT CASTELLANOS alias ROGELIO himself was arrested too.

2.- The plan of actions comprises:

a) Attempt on the Prime Minister's life. The MRR was planning an assassination plot of the Comrade Prime Minister FIDEL CASTRO.

b) Attempt on the so-called "Red Guard's life" (the CIA applied this term to old-guard revolutionary leaders of the PSP).

The MRR specifically planned assassination plots of the following comrades: DR. JUAN MARINELLO, BLAS ROCA, LÁZARO PEÑA and Commander FÉLIX TORRES.

c) The Responsibles of Actions in provinces are entrusted in order to make plans of sabotage, or attacks. For instance, we know that in Las Villas aerial photos and drawings of different military facilities were received through that via.

It was ordered to check main bridges of the province, indicating to use trustworthy engineers to find out the key points of the bridges.

It was planned to place touch mines in the pipe system transporting fuel, from ships to tanks in the Bay of Cienfuegos, using frogmen. It was planned the execution of a plan at Tallapiedra Plant from within (this was in Havana city) through personnel that had been searched in the plant.

Sabotage to all fuel facilities, fuel depots, Manacas brewery and transports were planned.

The preparation of this plan was calculated for five or six months.

d) In addition to the Bandit Factions in Las Villas and Matanzas, which were to be reinforced, the opening of a front in Pinar del Río and one—if possible—in Oriente, was planned.

The following measures were taken with that goal:

1) Sending two assistants, one of the Head of Faction JUAN JOSÉ CATALÁ COSTE also known as PICHI that operates in Matanzas, and other of MANUEL PACHECO RODRÍGUEZ, also known as CONGO, under arrest, who operated in Las Villas. Although this individual was arrested together with other three bandits, the rest is upraised under the command of LEONARDO PEÑATE MEDINA also known as EL CARNICERO [The Butcher]. Those two assistants left to be trained in "guerrillas" and "equipment reception," in order to later train their respective guerrillas. They were going to enter in the frustrated infiltration where we lost three comrades.

2) Contacts were established with the liaisons of PASTOR GONZÁLEZ alias CARA LINDA [Pretty Face], who operates in Pinar del Río.

3) Contacts are being made with the National Coordinator of the Martí Democratic Movement who said to have a group upraised in Oriente. In fact, he is trying to foster it.

e) The organization was restructured in such a way that it were less vulnerable to our penetration, eliminating Province Coordinators and some complete Sections. Later, there was a counterorder reestablishing the Province Coordinators, something logic and necessary for the integration with other organizations at that level.

    f) The MRR indicated to fix security points in big scale in all coasts for entrance and departure of speedboats with men, materiel, instructions, etc. A man was sent to be specifically trained in that aspect. After carrying out unity, the materiel would mainly arrive through the MRR, even though the other organizations were to receive a part. It is estimated a necessary forty-five-day term for the reception of equipments for the actions and for reinforcing Bandit Factions.

    g) The CIA gives too much importance to the establishment of an intelligence network. They ask reports of three kinds:

1) Economic

2) Military and

3) Public opinion from different parts of Cuba on the different measures implemented by the Revolution. Occasionally, the diplomatic baggage was used forsending the reports.

The MRR was giving steps aimed at both achieving agree ments with organizations and executing actions simulta neously. If the agreement was not accomplished, the MRR was to fulfill its part in the plan of action anyway.

b.- The former National Coordinator of the MRR, CARLOS BANDÍN LÓPEZ, and the former National Military Coordinator RICARDO A. CHÁVEZ SUÁREZ alias EL MEXICANO [Mexican], elaborated a plan that according to the General Coordinator JUAN FALCÓN ZANMAR, was rejected, or displaced. Such a plan contemplated: the sending of some infiltration groups equipped with radio-telegraphers. Such groups, made up of ten or twelve men, had two functions to fulfill:

    1.- Undertaking "command actions," being picked up to place them again in another territory using speedboats, or finally exfiltrate them to outside.

    2.- Settling in form of "guerrillas" to similarly act as the Bandit Factions, with the difference of self-supply through radio-telegraphy.

c.- Shortly after the USSR Declaration to stop intentions of imperialist aggression, bewilderment emerged amongst some Cuban and Yankee circles. The thesis of "pacific coexistence" emerged from that bewilderment, according to reports of the National Coordinator of the MRR, JUAN FALCÓN ZANMAR.

B.- Arrival of two agents of the Central Intelligence Agency to Cuba bound for the STUDENT REVOLUTIONARY DIRECTORATE, and their relations with the MRR.

A few weeks after arresting the leadership of the Revolutionary Recovery Movement, two agents of the CIA: JULIO HERNÁNDEZ ROJO and LUIS FERNANDO ROCHA RODRÍGUEZ infiltrate through a point in Varadero. The former was bound for the post of Military National Coordination and the latter for the post of the National General Coordination. The previous General Coordinator had been arrested during the dragnet to the MRR when we captured him in one of the houses having relations with both organizations.

The MRR and the DRE had always been very close, and particularly JUAN MANUEL GUILLOT CASTELLANOS developed countless activities accompanied by and with the collaboration of leaders of the Student Revolutionary Directorate.

We have backgrounds allowing us to assure that between the DRE (its leaders) and the ones of the MRR there was a close relation in many aspects. It is rare to see that two organizations had collaborated so closely, without arriving at any unity pact.

C.- Plans of the Central Intelligence Agency to be executed by the Student Revolutionary Directorate.

The organization named Student Revolutionary Directorate has the following features at present:

a.- It has an organization of national character. (Even though it is destroyed in Pinar del Río and Oriente.)

b.- Its leadership is made up of cadres, ideologically convinced, the majority of them from the University Catholic Grouping. Such cadres hold direction capability.

c.- This grouping is formed, in all levels, by young and daring elements, what ensures greater possibilities for undertaking actions.

d.- It has not received demolishing strikes. The sporadic arrests over its leadership are because of its cadres relations with the

MRR. With the "picking up" of the leadership, it is "justified" to believe that we have not penetrated the DRE.

e.- It has direct contact with imperialism.

f.- It holds training camps in the United States.

The existing characteristics in the MRR in the past were similar to those of the DRE at present. There was the difference that the MRR was nationally organized (except in Las Villas where it was recently destroyed and was being reconstructed), and that the MRR had not received strong strikes a long time ago.

It was in those moments (when the MRR had those special characteristics) that Imperialism provided all its cooperation, facilitating the MRR direct contact, training camps, infiltration speedboats, etc.

According to matters that JULIO HERNÁNDEZ ROJO has explained, and steps he has given in his activities, we can assure that the Student University Directorate, as a CIA instrument, plans to:

a.- Undertake some actions nationwide, particularly against the economy and big industries, to be executed in a single day: JULIO HERNÁNDEZ ROJO has requested a minimum of twenty actions per province, and the National Coordinator of Action and Sabotage has given instructions in that sense.

b.- Strengthen the Bandit Factions to perpetrate other simultaneous actions to the ones above-mentioned:

1.- To that purpose, JULIO HERNÁNDEZ ROJO sent some money to the Chief of Bandit Group in Matanzas, JUAN JOSÉ CATALÁ COSTE alias PICHI, as a gift, which was rejected, asking for ammunitions and weapons instead. JULIO HERNÁNDEZ is making contacts for an interview with that Bandit.

2.- Contacts with liaisons of the Chief of Bandit Group in Las Villas, JOSÉ MARTÍ CAMPOS alias CAMPITOS have been achieved.

In general, coordination and supply of all Bandit Groups, with weapons and sabotage means, is planned, so that the "X" day they launch actions together with those of the cities and infiltration groups.

c.- Massive training of infiltration groups: At present, the DRE has fifteen well-trained men in demolition and sabotage, ready to be gradually introduced in the country.

Apart from this, men who could run away when the Bay of Pigs have been chosen that, in addition to others taken out from a group of 2000 men who did not come then, make a total of 100, which are going to be infiltrated the "X" day, or a day before, through the same place, or through different places at once, who will undertake combined actions with the two previous kinds.

d.- Preparations of assassination plots: The National Coordinator of Actions has instructed groups of action the preparation of attempts on figures lives, without specifying who, but that has given orders to make checking to the individual the Chief of the Group "likes the most" in order to later present the plan and pass it.

e.- OAS intervention: For the "X" day, a general uprising in Latin America is planned, provoking strikes in different Latin American countries in support of actions against our Country. It is expected that in Miami streets be closed, and great riots take place, also asking for the OAS intervention. The tours that Miró Cardona carries out through Latin America at present may have relation with this point.

f.- The DRE is carrying out compartmentalization. Action and Sabotage, and Supplies will remain functioning in Havana, and the Province Coordinator will be eliminated. Likewise, the Intelligence Section was created. Countless changes have been made in National and Province posts everywhere, even changing the National Military Coordinator, JULIO HERNÁNDEZ ROJO, for the post of Supply National Coordinator. From that post, he will keep the same control of the Organization and will control different materiel as well.

g.- Defining points of security in coasts:

1.- JULIO HERNÁNDEZ ROJO instructed the search of a point in Las Villas for taking out the present National Coordinator, LUIS FERNÁNDEZ ROCHA RODRÍGUEZ in a fishing boat to be intercepted by an artillery speed-boat with a caliber 50, one 57-mm recoilless cannon, two Bar rifles and two Fal rifles. Two CIA agents would come in that travel to be in charge of the organization in Pinar del Río and Oriente, in addition to the telegrapher of the organization.

2.- HERNÁNDEZ ROJO has made contacts in Matanzas aimed at the search of points in the coasts.

In general, it can be stated that the order to search points has been nationawide. We have under control FERNÁNDEZ ROCHA's departure and we are having control of all obtained points.

h.- Establishment of intelligence network: JULIO HERNÁNDEZ ROJO appointed MANUEL SABAS NICOLAIDES alias ANGELITO, National Intelligence Coordinator, giving him broad instructions on the way to work and the kind of intelligence to be recollected. Reports are the same as those requested by the MRR.

i.- JULIO HERNÁNDEZ ROJO expressed to an agent that the DRE has a key they call Cayo Vaca, abandoned by the British, which is the operational base of the organization at present.

In order to better assess the importance that JULIO HERNÁNDEZ ROJO might be playing in imperialist plans, we should point out that he met with various Yankee Senators and Representatives, even he had lunch at the White House, although he never met with Kennedy, before coming to Cuba.

D.- Arrangements for unity that the so-called organizations: STUDENT REVOLUTIONARY DIRECTORATE, PEOPLE'S REVOLUTIONARY MOVEMENT, REVOLUTIONARY MOVEMENT NOVEMBER 30 "FRANK PAÍS," CHRISTIAN DEMOCRATIC MOVEMENT, REVOLUTIONARY UNITY MOVEMENT, and DEMOCRATIC REVOLUTIONARY RESCUE recently undertook.

Although we lack accurate data at the level where arrangements for accomplishing unity of the four biggest and remaining organizations, after disappearing the MRR leadership (MRP, DRE, MR-30-11, and MDC) are undertaken, we have indications that such arrangements have been continued, handling again the names of Revolutionary Unity and Democratic Revolutionary Rescue, which initially were going to be included, but JUAN MANUEL GUILLOT CASTELLANOS alias ROGELIO opposed. With his arrest, this obstacle seems no longer exist.

a.- On June 14, the National Coordinator of Revolutionary Unit, BERNARDO ÁLVAREZ PERDOMO also known as ROBERTO, moved to the area of Isabela de Sagua to contact fishermen, aimed at achieving their involvement in the reception of two CIA infiltration teams through that place, and departure

104

of two individuals, one of them the National Coordinator of the MRP, CHICHO.

b.- Through another way we know that the same day, JULIO HERNÁNDEZ ROJO and other DRE leaders interviewed with the Sagua DRE Coordinator, who has contact with the fisherman who leaves through that port, and will pick up the DRE National Coordinator and CIA agent, LUIS FERNÁNDEZ ROCHA RODRÍGUEZ, who will leave accompanied by the National Coordinator of the MRP, CHICHO.

c.- A letter, apparently written by the National Coordinator of Democratic Revolutionary Rescue, was intercepted. There it is pointed out the entrance of an individual in Cuba who has no links with counterrevolutionary organizations, and who made the same statements as JUAN MANUEL GUILLOT CASTELLANOS on unity, restructuring, province grouping, etc., including Democratic Revolutionary Rescue.

Immediately after he says (the person who writes the letter) that he made contact with MR-30-11, MDC, and Unity to sign with them without the MRP.

d.- Almost simultaneously with this letter, dated on June 7, 1962, a manifesto "To the Cuban People" signed by CHRISTIAN DEMOCRATIC MOVEMENT, DEMOCRATIC REVO- LUTIONARY RESCUE, REVOLUTIONARY MOVEMENT NOVEMBER 30 "FRANK PAÍS," and REVOLUTIONARY UNITY MOVEMENT, appears, where it is stated that such organizations have gotten together in the so-called Revolution- ary National Board.

e.- Two weeks ago the Civil National Coordinator of the MR-30-11 expressed that he had signed the unity between the MR-30-11, DRE, and MRP. This has not been confirmed.

f.- Because of a case in Oriente Province, it was detected that on June 9, the unity of the MR-30-11, MRP, DRE, FRD, and MDR had been signed, and that they were going to function in the provinces in the Island; making the decision that in the case of Camagüey and Oriente provinces, five coordinators would work, one was to be the Commander in Chief and the other four were to be the Captain Coordinators.

SPECIAL REPORT[1]

---

1. Excerpt of the original paper, Ministry of the Interior.

REPUBLICA DE CUBA

MINISTERIO DEL INTERIOR

DPTO. SEGURIDAD DEL ESTADO

CONTENTS

WE SHALL OVERCOME

MINISTERIO DEL INTERIOR

DPTO. SEGURIDAD DEL ESTADO

Havana, January 17, 1963
Year of Organization

From : Minister of the Interior
To : National Directorate of the ORI
Subject : On imperialist tactics and strategy. Increase of the internal counterrevolutionary activity. Increase of banditry. Policy of infiltration and isolation of Cuba.

The activity of the counterrevolutionary organizations and leaders outside of Cuba were to reveal, one more time, the state of decadence and lack of unity that reigned in the counterrevolutionary ranks. The main of the contradictions was to be showed within the same Assault Brigade 2506, based on the statement of Enrique Llaca, Jr., exposed last week, on the excessive ambitions of the "leaders" in the exile, which also were considered as elements lacking ideals, and concluded stating the dissolution of the Assault Brigade 2506 for having fulfilled its goals.

This declaration was responded by the "leadership" of the Brigade, made up of Artime and company, stating that it was a military organization, and as such, were "on furlough" at the moment.

Seemingly, not even Kennedy's statements calling the *gusanos*[2] to achieve unity succeeded in smoothing things over in the campaigns of the "battle of Miami." Amongst the counterrevolutionary organizations, there were deep and hard contradictions not to be easily resolved.

In spite of the above-mentioned contradiction, emerged in the heart of the mercenary brigade, Imperialism, and Yankee agencies, continued giving all their propaganda and effective support to it. In late week, it

---

2. This is the word the Cubans use to name the counterrevolutionaries, since the very beginning of the Revolution. It means "worm." *Ed.*

was mentioned the visit of members of the mercenary headquarters to Washington to meet with the Attaché of Cuban Affairs, Sterlin J. Cottrell, whom Kennedy recently appointed to coordinate plans concerning Cuba. Public information mentioned that the goal of the mercenaries travel was to present a plan on Cuba.

Through a confidential intelligence, received during the week, in a source linked to the top leadership of the counterrevolution, the unitary catalyst role that Yankees had assigned to mercenaries of the "2506," as well as the leading role of Artime in it, was cited again. It was reported that this was the contact between the internal counterrevolutionary elements with the external ones, as well as that contact was in charge of introducing the materiel, explosives and other equipments in the country. Prior confidential intelligence pointed to Artime as the main element within the group of mercenaries.

Plans of Aggressions

The last confidential intelligence received through our different means and sources outside on the enemy activity inside and outside of Cuba, as well as the analyses of intelligence appeared in public source on imperialist plans and attitudes against our Revolution, were shaping an attack strategic plan, which agreed in pointing out the counterrevolutionary infiltration activity from outside for sabotage, opening of bandit fronts, piracy attacks, and increase and variation in inside elements activity.

All facts above mentioned impose the undertaking of a special report on the ultimate received intelligence concerning the infiltration line.

New Conceptions of the Pentagon

Changes brought about by the Kennedy administration in the functioning and structure of the Yankee Armed Forces are aimed at the purpose of Imperialism to face the present international policy situation, and within this, to two main facts: the increase of liberation movement and the advance of the Socialist Bloc.

The main ideologist of these new strategic theories of the Pentagon, General Maxwell Taylor, military advisor of Kennedy and newly appointed Chief of the Board of Joint Chiefs of Staff, considers the new theory as "flexible strategy," basically consisting in that the United States should be capable of reacting before any possible challenge and act before any situation.

112

Amongst the main points of the "flexible strategy" it is mentioned a new conception of local war. This is interpreted as any conflict in which the United States as a nation is not directly threatened.

In this theory, special wars are included, that is, guerrilla and anti-guerrilla operations. By special war it is interpreted every war that means military actions through non-conventional means.

It must be taken into account that these elements, together with bodies of intelligence of the State Department and other agencies of the Yankee Government, are the ones in charge of undertaking aggressive projects of the Imperialism against our Revolution.

Infiltration Policy

According to a study undertaken on intelligence prior the Cuban Missile Crisis aimed at determining characteristics of training camps and aggressive policy followed by Yankees and the counterrevolutionary organizations outside of Cuba, and concluded on November 10, 1962, the following data were obtained:

1.- It was started to perceive, with special strength in confidential intelligence, a strong trend to denounce infiltration activities.

2.- Concerning the training camps of mercenaries in Central America, it was pointed out that together with the presence of others for conventional-type training, there were "special tasks," guerrilla warfare, sabotage and attempts of assassination. It was particularly mentioned the presence of foreign trainers, mainly Chinese and Japanese, specialized in such functions.

Intelligence pointed out the sending of one of these groups to the Naval Base of Guantánamo. Together with this was mentioned the use of Cuban counterrevolutionaries, former officials specialized in tasks of training Latin American soldiers in Yankee academies of guerrilla warfare, while presenting them in the role of trained individuals in these tasks and, particularly, in infiltration tasks.

3.- From the analysis of the intelligence received in the Department on training camps in areas of Florida, through different confidential and public sources, clearly appeared that in this area, there were no big training camps, but small, in houses and farms devoted to train elements for infiltration of three, or four elements.

In that sense, infiltration elements arrested by the State Security Department (DSE) in the area of Caibarién, in Las Villas in July, had declared.

As the enemy advanced in the development of its plans, evidences of them were greater, both public and confidential. All these activities took a special significance when the mercenaries of the Bay of Pigs leave the country, a fact with which a new phase of Yankee aggression plans on Cuba was to be initiated, according to various intelligence was going to prove it.

The early mention of future activities of counterrevolutionary elements both inside and outside of Cuba, in the new role that Imperialism assigned to them, appear in an UPI cable information, dated on December 30, in which, together with an indication that a long-term new policy was about to be initiated on the Castro-Communist regime, some points referred in the indicated policy were mentioned. Special importance, amongst others, was given to:

1.- Preference for economic and political pressure through the OAS.

2.- Acceleration of underground activities inside of Cuba, including also the possibility to provide "political encouragement," but not military, to Cuban refugees, in order to help their people to defeat the Fidel Castro-Communist regime.

This first cable was to be the first link of a well-elaborated enemy campaign, in which the main elements were to be the released mercenaries and public activity of the Yankee authorities on Cuba, above all aimèd at creating a propitious atmosphere for restrictive measures from the economic and political viewpoint.

Intelligence and infiltration activities increased. After the release of the cable above mentioned, some confidential-type intelligence begins to arrive through different sources, proving the enemy activity aimed at attacking and infiltrating saboteur elements.

1.- In mid-December intelligence, it is pointed out that the Liberation Army proposed recruiting 1000 men for undertaking guerrilla activities in the mountains of Oriente, Las Villas and Pinar del Río. They would land by sea.

Concerning bandit and internal counterrevolutionary organization activities, it was pointed out that there were plans aimed at increasing new bandit groups.

2.- Through a source of confidence, linked to CIA infiltration elements, it was indicated that the CIA must have carried out more than fifteen travels to Cuba between April and October 1962, in order to introduce weapons, explosives, and propaganda in Cuba. That after cessation of the blockade, Yankees had instructed them to end the sending of weapons.

114

3.- . . . it was known that in diplomatic and journalist circles of this city Kennedy's speech had been taken as an order for initiating, or reinforcing actions on our country, expecting that such actions were undertaken through OAS actions against Cuban trade, pirate raids, sabotage, and subversive activities.[3]

4.- . . . intelligence was received on undertaking of attacks on the part of Alpha 66 organization against our coasts. The main target of the attack would be refineries and fuel depots. CIA agents, infiltrated in Cuba, were to support this action. Following the facts, the counterrevolutionary organization DRE would be in charge of carrying out a violent press campaign demanding fulfillment of inter-American agreements in order to complete the multilateral action.

Intelligence came from different sources, some of these from Latin American countries, the rest from the United States. Even in the case of Yankee intelligence, relation between them was impossible, what determines that the phenomenon was noted in all spheres of the counterrevolution, from journalist and diplomatic circles of Washington to the basis of counterrevolutionary organizations.

Through State Security means various findings of war materiel and explosives typical of infiltrated elements in different areas of the country, as well as the arrest of a group of these elements, were to be carried out.

Together with data on infiltration and in many occasions as intelligence elements of them, also the enemy plans aimed at undertaking pirate attacks were underlined. Main intelligence on this fact was received from sources of our confidence. Of these, we should mention the following:

1.- . . . it was known of a leadership meeting of ones of these groups with DRE elements. This meeting mainly dealt with plans of attacks of pirate speedboats of Alpha 66 (this report appears mentioned in the previous point 4).

In this case, targets of attacks against our country are pointed out. According to intelligence, these were focussed on destruction of refineries and fuel depots in La Habana, Cienfuegos, and Santiago de Cuba. That is, attacks are mainly aimed at national economy.

2.- In a very trustworthy information . . . was mentioned that the organization Alpha 66 was planning to continue attacks against Cuba.

3. The ellipsis points—in this case and in the subsequent ones in this report—indicate that part of the source text has not been declassified. *Ed.*

Also it pointed out the activity of other counterrevolutionary organizations aimed at carrying out attacks against our coasts, without defining concrete targets in these cases. Amongst these, plans of DRE, together with the Liberation Army to carry out this kind of aggression, were mentioned. Another report was pointing out that it was planned attacking, or bombarding Havana in early February. The organization, or organizations involved in this attack were not mentioned.

All this activity denounced by confidential intelligence on pirate attacks against our coasts, was to subsequently be known through the very counterrevolutionary organizations, particularly in the case of Alpha 66, which in public statements underlined its intention to continue attacks against Cuba.

Because of its content and exposition, statements of leaders of this organization were an important element of confirmation for confidential intelligence, because they were formed with the denounced points in them on prohibition of such actions from the Yankee territory.

Subsequently, in the late week, a statement of a counterrevolutionary group headed by Roberto Parson was received. There he said that they carried out an aggression against our coasts in the past months, resulting in two kidnapped militiamen. The referred organization also stated that they were to carry out attacks on our country, even though they would not have to be based on the Yankee territory.

New Tactical Line of Imperialism

This new line concretely pointed out the following matters:

1.- The impossibility of carrying out a counterrevolutionary armed aggression—with success—on the Cuban Revolution without effective support of the U.S. armed forces; even if the army is better prepared and organized than that of the Bay of Pigs.

It is unlikely that this may occur for the moment due to the international situation.

Almost all the counterrevolutionary organizations outside of Cuba and, particularly, the Council that Miró Cardona chairs, sustain the above-mentioned line of Yankee support for an aggression. Different leaders of that organization had expressed themselves, more than once, in favor of the direct-armed aggression on our revolution as the only choice to achieve the "liberation." In that sense, the several statements made by Tony Varona, and the last ones by Miró Cardona abound, giving their support to any kind of direct, or collective aggression on Cuba.

2.- In view of the above-mentioned, the counterrevolutionary forces should propose the following main tasks:

a) Organizing subversive activities inside of Cuba.

b) Incursions on Cuba should be aimed at damaging the economy and military facilities. This requires a greater preparation of incursions from outside.

3.- Internal counterrevolutionary activities should consider the following aspects:

a) Guerrilla activity in the mountains should be adequate for undertaking subversive and sabotage actions in cities and agricultural areas, largely populated.

This activity has the advantage of being the most effective method for demoralizing the population and attracting public attention on guerrilla actions taking place at present.

Through the State Security Department (DSE) means, diverse changes in guerrilla tactics for the last weeks have been reported in Cuba. These changes probably took place as an abandonment of low areas to go into mountainous ones. Subsequently, a reverse phenomenon took place, which is placing us before tactical retreat, mainly aimed at coordinating and grouping forces again in order to undertake new tasks. Meetings for such a purpose were carried out, and plans to seize again low areas and open guerrilla fronts in other areas, which have the characteristics above-mentioned in intelligence, subsequently took place. . . .

Artime Role

The received report pointed out that the mercenary Artime was the main contact between the external and internal counterrevolution, and the element in charge of introducing materiel and propaganda in Cuba.

Also, it was stated the use of Yankee reconnaissance planes for this infiltration activity, or dropping weapons in the national territory.

As it is easily observed, the received report was confirming, one by one, the points previously detected and already mentioned at the beginning of it, on what the plans of imperialism were and the means that are being prepared for carrying out such a task.

As element of special importance and highly revealing we can mention the recent appointment, by Kennedy, of a Special Committee for Cuba, made up of an specialist on anti-guerilla affairs, who has been in charge of the Office for South Viet-Nam Affairs, Sterling Contrell. It should be pointed out the recent meeting between elements of the mercenary Assault Brigade of the Bay of Pigs and the above-mentioned

Yankee specialist, in order to discuss and present their plans on new tasks in Cuba.

Diverse facts of special importance and significance in further defensive activities of our Revolution follow from the analysis of all intelligence previously exposed. These can be summarized in the following points:

1.- Through intelligence and the most diverse confidential sources, without contact amongst them, it is pointed out that Yankee imperialism maintains public campaigns against the Revolution; and finally, that there is a defined line of attack on our Revolution according to news of the inside counterrevolution itself:

a) Enemy activity aimed at infiltrating counterrevolutionary elements for undertaking specific tasks of sabotage on the economy and military targets.

b) Use of bandits operating in different areas of the country for committing command and pirate attacks, and reinforcement of them with external (infiltrated) elements, as well as economic and military support to them.

c) Use of pirate boats and command attacks on our coasts aimed at carrying out sabotage.

All the above-mentioned is mainly aimed at creating a state of internal disturbances to allow fostering an international atmosphere favorable for collective intervention against our country.

Delaying and destroying economic plans of the Revolution aimed at presenting the failure of it.

In general, we can state that the United States is getting ready now to begin a truly "special war." The external and internal counterrevolutionary elements will carry out this war.

The special war of imperialism against our Revolution is inexcusably accompanied by diverse diplomatic and political steps with which they pretend to create a real siege to our economic activities and of all kind.

This is, finally, the conception that the present administration has concerning war, as a means of domination and destruction of revolutions and movements of national liberation. That is why the plans denounced here are the main strategic goal at present.

Being these its conceptions, it is consistent that they try to develop these conceptions against its main enemy at present: the Cuban Revolution, which undoubtedly is a fact of far-reaching importance in the world history, as the beginning of Latin America liberation is.

This general line detected outside of Cuba, subdued to the reality of facts developing in Cuba, is perfectly proved. The operation of internal counterrevolution and that of imperialist infiltrated agents, which, are really, the ones in charge of putting into practice that general line, are synchronized.

Increase of Internal Counterrevolutionary Activity

The actions registered in the last weeks indicate that there is an increasing trend in the internal counterrevolutionary activity, particularly, in the fronts of sabotage to economy and banditry.

It is convenient to analyze, although superficially, the enemy activity in July, August, and September, that is, during the pre-crisis period. From the first of the above-mentioned months, a trend to drop in counterrevolutionary attack is found out.

For instance, in July, 185 actions in the whole country were recorded, while in August, the reports state 82 undertaken acts.

When comparing activities between July and September, a considerable decrease, both in quantity and in quality of attacks, is observed. The difference between both periods is 103 fewer actions registered in the last month.

The intense phase of the crisis can be located between October 16 and November 26. During this six-week period, seventy-one actions were reported, forty-seven of them, directed to economy and mainly on sugar cane. In this front, twenty-six fires took place, with a total of 73,200 arrobas[4] burned.

Never before, up to this date, there had ever been so a low counterrevolutionary activity, because the average was eleven actions per week.

From the lifting of the blockade, a trend to increase the counterrevolutionary activity begins to be outlined, specially reflected in:

a) Increase of attacks in the economic front, particularly in the burning of sugar-cane plantations.

b) Increase of bandit movement, practically inactive during the crisis.

c) Intensification of infiltration policy, using in the majority of the cases the Naval Base of Guantánamo as starting point to introduce spies in the territory.

---

4. One arroba equals 25 pounds. Ed.

d) Efforts of the counterrevolutionary organizations in order to organize and reorganize, to provide assistance to factions, to seek contacts outside and attempts of unity.

e) Revival of counterrevolutionary activity by religious sects, specially standing out the Jehovah's Witnesses and the Gideon's Band. Some priests of the Catholic Church are conspiring and even recollecting explosives and other materiel to commit sabotage acts. It is also known of a priest who is the liaison between undetermined counterrevolutionary organizations and embassies.

Confirmation of these enemy trends is found in the following facts:

1.- Between November 27 and December 17, seventy-three counterrevolutionary actions were recorded. That is, during the pre-crisis period, the enemy committed an average of eleven attacks per week; once the blockade was lifted, the percentage increased to twenty-four actions per week.

During the subsequent weeks, the trend to increase became clearer. Between December 18 and 26, thirty actions were registered; in the following week ninety-five, and in the last week, ninety-three.

Following data clearly underline the increase of counterrevolutionary activity. During the nine weeks between October 16 and December 17, a total 144 actions were reported. The weekly average was of sixteen actions.

During the three following weeks, 218 actions of the counterrevolution took place. The weekly average increased to seventy-two actions.

Moreover, in the quality of actions there was a considerable variation. For example:

2.- Of the 218 counterrevolutionary actions recorded in the last three weeks, 98 took place in sugar-cane plantations. The amount of arrobas burned was 1,106,423.

Intensification of counterrevolutionary operation in cane fields responds to a general plan, nationally detected in the field of banditry and in the majority of the counterrevolutionary organizations.

The attack on the sugar industry is aimed at damaging the most important branch of our economy. Sugar cane means hard currency. Last year, all records of cane burning were outdone when burning more than 305 million arrobas, what meant a sensitive loss in hard currency.

3.- Other nineteen attacks on cattle-raising and agriculture took place in the country. This means that more than a half of the counterrevolutionary action was carried out in rural areas. For instance, fire destroyed 250 tons of hay, 8 chicken barns devoted to chicken breeding were burned in a farm in San Nicolás de Bari, where 35,000 chickens died and two houses were reduced to ashes.

It can also be mentioned the destruction of five tobacco houses and poisoning of dammed water in a cooperative of small farmers in Sancti Spíritus.

4.- Changes in quality of sabotage is also observed in urban areas. The enemy was not acting in factories for so long. During this period, a match's factory and other for manufacturing dolls were destroyed by fire. It is estimated that this has to do with two sabotages, aspect that is being checked at present.

Also, persistence in plans of sabotage on refineries maintained, there was an attempt to set fire in two movie-theaters and a plan to set fire in a garment store was found out.

Another aspect of the intensification of attack on the economy and change of quality that we talked about is reflected in sabotage to transport. Aside of some derailments under investigation at present, two typical cases of sabotage that are being carried out in this sector can be pointed out, for instance:

a) At Cruces, when checking locomotives No. 61 and 603, screws and washers were found in the oiling box, what had not ever been found out would have ruined both machines.

b) At Terminal No. 31 of the Cuban Petroleum Institute (ICP) in Matanzas emery powder was found out in a tray with oil for fuel trucks. This act would have left unused all engines of trucks, which are supplied in the above-mentioned terminal.

The activity of the counterrevolution collected in this paragraph expresses that the rising trend remains and that quality has suffered a variation.

Banditry Movement

Action of bands in all the country seems to respond to an organized plan and it is indicating that some progress has been made respecting unity of bands.

According to evidences known by the DSE, it is concluded that trends in this front of the counterrevolution are the following:

1.- Joining bands operating in Las Villas and Camagüey, something that seems to be achieved under the command of Tomás San Gil. This unity is aimed at opening the so-called Northern Front in Yaguajay area. It was known that a band from that area is going to Remedios-Zuluetas region, with instructions to set fire sugar canes of Zaza and San José sugar mills.

Also, it is sought to spread bandit groups in Camagüey Province, in the most organized way.

It was also detected that heads of bands in Matanzas and Las Villas provinces are getting ready for a meeting on the 20th in order to join banditry actions from La Habana to Camagüey provinces.

2.- Opening new fronts in Oriente Province, above all, in Baracoa, Guantánamo, Yateras, and Sagua de Tánamo boroughs. The important presence of the Naval Base of Guantánamo in this province plays a role in these purposes.

3.- Reinforcing bands through material assistance of the counter-revolutionary organizations operating in the boroughs.

An example of this is the relation established between bands and organizations such as in the cases of RCA, UNIR, JAR, MRR, M-30-11, and others.

4.- Instructions to the bands to spread terror amongst revolutionary elements in areas where they operate. Examples that are directed in that sense are the following:

a) Assault on the house of the militiaman Agapito González Montanar in San Antonio de las Vegas. After setting fire to the house, they shot at its dwellers; González Montanar was wounded. Without a brake, a milking stable at Añilito farm, 445 yards away from the place previously mentioned was set on fire, where the eleven-year-old boy, Leopoldo Martínez Rodríguez was killed.

b) Assault on the house of the campesino José Ramón Palacios, in a place known as El Corojal, Trinidad. José Ramón Palacios was killed; a son and a grandson wounded.

c) Murder of the forest police officer Jesús Sardiñas Álvarez, attacked by a bandit group in the camp where he worked in Aguada de Pasajeros. After being wounded, he was sprayed with gas-oil and set fire.

5.- Intensify attacks on farming production, mainly to cane sugar production. For instance, it is known that the bandit Pichi Catalá has ordered to set fire to huge amounts of transporters, tilters, and everything that can be useful for cane-sugar production.

These are the trends, but a small analysis of the forces that banditry counts on and the way they are distributed must be done. It should make emphasis that figures are not completely accurate, and they respond to intelligence that the DSE has up to date.

The total of bands reported are 70, gathering at about 589 bandits. The distribution is as follows:

a) Pinar del Río three groups, with approximately fifteen bandits;

b) In La Habana, two bands with thirteen bandits. In this case it should be pointed out that it deals of a remaining group that was operating in Jaruco, who are upraised for more than a year. This group had not operated and in the last days it has undertaken three attacks;

c) In Matanzas, fifteen, with an average of eighty-two bandits;

d) In Las Villas, 40 bands have been reported, made up of 433 bandits approximately;

e) In Camagüey, four with twenty-nine bandits;

f) In Oriente five are reported, with seventeen bandits.

During the pre-crisis period, that is, in July, August, and September, the factions committed fifty-one attacks, but were strongly stricken, because the revolutionary forces could fight forty combats, which resulted in fifty-six captured bandits and twenty-eight dead. . . . In this figure, it must be taken into account that many of them were imprisoned before July, the period contemplated in this report.

From November to date, the bands have carried out fifty-eight attacks. It must be emphasized that out of those actions, thirty-one were carried out between December 18 and January 11, that is, in less than a month.

Contrasting with the period passed between July and September, encounters carried out between November and January 11, increase to five. Captured bandits are twenty-two and dead in combat are twenty-four. . . .

Statistics previously exposed make us conclude:

1- That in the pre-crisis period, covering three months, the bands carried out seven attacks less than in the second period, which covers just two months.

2- That in the first period, revolutionary forces could fight forty combats, bandits suffered serious casualties, because it must be taken into account that important heads at the time, such as Benjamín Tardío, Arnoldo Martínez Andrade, Sancti Spíritus and other ringleaders died, while in the second period thirty-five less combats were registered. As logical outcome, the balance of captured and dead bandits was lower in three and thirty-four respectively.

3- That increase of band activities in this second period is not only checked with the exposition in the above-mentioned paragraphs, but also in the progress to join the commands that we have already talked about, something seemingly achieved in Las Villas and Camagüey. The fact of having met seventy men, amongst them the most important ringleaders of banditry, at a point of the Escambray, is telling about the strength that they have accomplished and the relative impunity they are moving with.

In short, the counterrevolutionary activity and banditry action during last week confirm the trend to the increase and changes in quality of the enemy operation. Let us see the of actions the ultimate week:

a) Fifty-five sugar-cane fires, with a total of 440,975 burned arrobas were registered. In this occasion, Camagüey and Las Villas were the most affected provinces with 160,360 and 142,607 arrobas burned respectively. Matanzas followed those provinces with 121,908. It must be clarified that there were cane burns all over the provinces.

b) Twelve-bandit attacks were reported, three in La Habana, one in Matanzas, and eight in Las Villas. In one of those attacks, reported in Matanzas Province, bandits killed two members of the Committee for Revolutionary Instruction (COR).

c) In another attack that took place at Camilo Cienfuegos farm, Guasimal neighborhood, Sancti Spíritus, fifteen bandits set fire different storehouses where jeeps and grain planters were stored. They also burned a store and an office, forcing three peasant families to see the attack.

d) On January 16, a group of sixteen bandits intercepted a train in Fomento. Because they could not burn the train, it was shot, and the machinist was forced to return back to the station. The militiamen and responsible of Wilfredo Cabrera farm, José González Pazo, and the responsible of livestock of the same farm, Ismael Alfonso Perera, were kidnapped. Their bodies were found subsequently. The former's tongue and hands were cut, and the latter's eyes were pulled out by shooting. Both were riddled with bullets holes.

e) It is important to underline the fire that took place in the vicinity of Melanio Hernández (Tuinicú) sugar mill, in Sancti Spíritus, where fire destroyed four train wagons. This can be related with something detected in Matanzas concerning the order that the head of bandits, Pichi Catalá had given to his bands in order to burn and destroy sugar-cane fields, transporters, tilters and everything that could affect the sugar industry.

f) Other ten sabotages in the agrarian sector were reported from Pinar del Río and Las Villas. Three additional fires developed in La Habana. Finally, a train collision was reported in Matanzas due to neglect. In the collision several persons were wounded.

It must be underlined the fire that destroyed the store for selling tires and recovered-tires at 510, Vives Street, in Havana city. Fire lasted several hours; firemen and members of the Public Order Department

(DOP) had to be assisted due to asphyxia, having arrested three individuals as presumed authors of this sabotage.

Total amount of counterrevolutionary actions was eighty-seven, of which, sixty-eight took place in rural areas.

The last week was separated from the rest of the report in order to make emphasis in the maintenance of the increase of counterrevolutionary activity, particularly, that of banditry, because of the fifty-five fires in sugar-cane fields, a vast majority were committed by those groups.

There are antecedents on this activity, particularly in Las Villas. It has been proved that fires, which took place in the farms Covadonga, Aniano Amador's property; San Rafael, Palacio de la Coba brothers' property; and the Ocuje, Felipe Pérez González's property, located in Aguada de Pasajeros, were the result of the owners action linked to bandits who operate in the area. The arrest of these elements has been ordered.

Increase of Espionage Activity

The noticed increase in infiltration policy, closely linked to action on economic front and banditry activity, should be underlined.

From the second half of December up to date, more than fifteen possible infiltrations of weapons and men have been reported. Many of them have been completely checked.

The areas where enemy actions are more often reported are: Guanahacabibes Peninsula; northern region of Las Villas, from Sagua to Quemado de Güines, mainly; Santa Cruz del Sur coast, in Camagüey, and finally, Baracoa, Guantánamo and other northern and southern points in Oriente Province.

The location of the Naval Base at Guantánamo in this province represents the most important beachhead of imperialism for this kind of activity.

From the date already mentioned, weapons and other objects have been found, what proves the possibility of infiltrations. They have been found in the following areas:

a) In Jutía Cay, north of Pinar del Río Province.

b) In Río del Indio, and Playa Baja, northern coast of the same province, in Viñales area.

c) In Malas Aguas Bay, in the same region. Last November Miguel Ángel Orozco infiltrated through this place.

Aerial and maritime violations have been reported through all these areas, supposing that much of them has relation with this infiltration policy.

125

d) On December 15, a mobile radio, fatigues, and weapons were seized at Carahatas Beach, in Quemado de Güines.

e) On the 16th a cargo of materiel was seized at Cayo Punta de los Pinos, north of Isabela de Sagua.

f) In Santiago Cay, in the same area, a small-and-silent boat with an outboard motor, one rubber lighter and other objects were seized.

g) In Manatí Cay, in San Francisco farm, in Carahatas; in El Salto Beach, in Corralillo; in the coast of Isleta farm, in Yaguajay, and in other many places of Las Villas Province traces of weapons and spies infiltrations have been found.

Confirming the fact that the infiltration policy through the northern part of Las Villas has notably intensified should be underlined the detected intelligence that the ringleader Méndez Esquijarrosa—attaché of Tomás Gil—stated that through Caibarién eight spies had penetrated to integrate the different bands.

h) Fully unconfirmed news on infiltrations through several tidelands that the coast is plagued with, have been received from Santa Cruz del Sur. Catalina planes landing on water, and submarines approaching near the coast to leave spies and to pick up men, have been seen. Finally, the presence of helicopters in several occasions in the area of Francisco del Guayabal has been reported.

i) The most recent case in the far east of Cuba led to the arrest of seventy-six liaisons who were working for five agents infiltrated through a point known as La Costa Beach, 700 meters off the Base border.

Aside of seizing weapons and other artifacts for spies tasks, it was confirmed that the group, directly under the command of the Base, was aimed at provoking uprisings in Chivirico, Ramón de las Yaguas, Filipinas, Baracoa, Sagua de Tánamo, Yateras, Guantánamo, Caney and Alto Songo.

During the past year, it was learned of several infiltrations coming from the Base, for instance: Amancio Mosqueda's—better known as Yarey—, Santiago Vegas Díaz and José Miguel Delgado Martínez's, and finally Julio Wright Simon's.

Emphasis should be made on the close relation between infiltration policy and the Base of Caimanera.[5] It should be remembered that CIA agents who have their operation station in such a place, prepared attempts on Commanders Fidel and Raúl Castro's lives.

---

5. This is the other name by which the Naval Base of Guantánamo is known in Cuba, due to the town close to the Base. *Ed.*

Recently it was learned that nineteen leaders of the counterrevolutionary organization Alpha 66, were there in the first ten days of December, in order to coordinate plans of actions, mainly attacks of pirate boats.

The detected activities, which reflect the enemy trend in that area, can be pointed out as follows:

1.- The agreement to take out the refugees in small groups for bases outside of Cuba, in order to train them and then infiltrate them into the national territory. That agreement was taken on December 31 with Bill Abbott, Luis Frías, and Roberto Escandón's involvement, the two latter were refugees in the Base, and a Captain of the Intelligence Service, surnamed Wilson.

This purpose was detected through another via, learning that one of the leaders expressed that this was a serious movement, whose Chief off Staff was in Miami and was backed by the CIA, having men and ships entering and leaving the country very often.

2.- Transferring constantly refugees to Jamaica, Haiti, and Puerto Rico, in groups of fifteen and twenty men. On January 8, 109 persons departed; all with the purpose to train for different tasks on Cuba.

3.- Reports on introduction of weapons in the national territory. It was learned that during the week of December 18-25, two grenade boxes, and eight rifles M-14 were to be introduced, to join them to other weapons. These would be taken out in a speedboat to be delivered to a bandit group somewhere in the coast.

Permanence of counterrevolutionary leaders, such as: Nino Díaz, Calzadilla, Balbuena, Elbo Torres, and others, in different phases, are symptoms of what the Base represents in developing activities on our country.

Finally, due to the facts accounted in this report, it is obvious the role that the Base plays as guiding, organizing and executing center, sometimes, in subversion plans. As conclusion it can be underlined:

a) The existing interrelation between counterrevolutionary organizations, bands, and the outside enemy, whose operational stations are Miami and the Naval Base of Guantánamo.

b) According to the relation made, it seems that attacks on the economic front, increase of banditry, intensification of the policy to introduce spies, revival of counterrevolutionary activity of religious sects, etc., are better linked and synchronized, that is, it seems, according to its sequence, to be a plan prepared by the CIA. The goal, of course, is weakening the internal front and creating, thus, conditions for the aggression.

Main Crimes Committed by Counterrevolutionary Groups during the Operation Mongoose

01/09/62   CAMPESINO WOUNDED

The campesino Cresencio Martell García was wounded at La Rosa rural estate, Agramonte, Matanzas, by Pedro "Perico" Sánchez González's band.

01/15/62   CAMPESINOS KILLED

The campesino Valentín Alonso Maceda and his son Valentín Alonso Barrera were killed when their house at El Naranjito rural estate, south of El Nicho, Escambray, was assaulted by Jesús Ramón "Realito" Real Hernández's band.

02/04/62   CAMPESINO KILLED

Francisco "Machete" Robaina Domínguez's band killed the campesino Dionisio Chirino in Taco Taco neighborhood, Candelaria, Pinar del Río.

02/12/62   CAMPESINOS WOUNDED

The campesino Gilberto Pérez and his wife Flora Guzmán were wounded when Francisco "Machete" Robaina Domínguez's band assaulted their house.

02/14/62   MILITIAMAN KILLED AND WOUNDED PEOPLE

The militiaman Bartolo Vázquez was killed, and his brother José Antonio and his nephew Félix Vázquez were gravely wounded by a counterrevolutionary band at Pulido rural estate, Alquízar, La Habana.

02/16/62   WORKER KILLED

Arnoldo Martínez Andrade's band killed the worker Orestes Bravo Rabí, before his relatives, in the second assault that the

128

band carries out to Perea asphalt mines, in Yaguajay borough, Sancti Spíritus.

02/17/62 CAMPESINO KILLED

Francisco "Machete" Robaina Domínguez's band killed the campesino Bernardino Álvarez at Laborí rural estate, Candelaria, Pinar del Río.

02/19/62 CAMPESINO KILLED

The campesino Manuel Quintana Tejera was killed at Malechal rural estate, near San Gregorio sugar-mill settlement, Manguito, Matanzas.

02/25/62 KILLING AND WOUNDED PEOPLE

Osirio Borges Rojas's band killed Pedro Carpio Cruz and wounded several persons in an attack to a ball in Sopimpa, Fomento, Sancti Spíritus.

03/03/62 KILLING

The counterrevolutionary band, under the command of Orlando de Armas Hernández, killed Francisco Rodríguez Rodríguez at Morejón rural estate, Bolondrón, Matanzas.

03/13/62 BOY KILLED

Bandit group killed the boy Andrés Rojas Açosta and fired the house of campesinos Ángel Rojas and Obdulia Rojas, father and sister of the boy, respectively, at Chicharrón rural estate, Jobo neighborhood, San Nicolás de Bari, La Habana.

03/13/62 KILLINGS AND BURNING OF SCHOOL, TOWN'S STORE, AND SOCIAL CLUB

The band, under the command of Arnoldo Martínez Andrade and Mario Bravo Cervantes, killed campesinos José María Padrón Melquía and Manuel Solís Díaz at Mártires de Bella Mota farm, Las Llanadas rural estate, Mayajigua neighborhood, Yaguajay. The town's store, the house of the social club, a school and several houses were burned.

03/23/62 WORKERS KILLED

The workers of Public Works Julio Rodríguez Utra and Sabino Hernández Romero were killed at Curva del Muerto, Trinidad-Topes de Collantes road. The bandits Benjamín "Pangüín" Tardío Hernández, José "Cheíto" León Jiménez, and Alfredo Amarantes "Maro" Borges Rodríguez, were involved in the killings.

03/27/62 WORKERS KILLED

Benjamín "Pangüín" Tardío Hernández's band killed Bombino Hernández and Enríquez Rodríguez when were placed as blocks in the wheels of a truck of Public Works that was gunshot in Sancti Spíritus.

03/30/62　Campesino killed and wounded people

The campesino José "Macho" Sierra Pacheco was killed, and Modesto Quesada Hernández and Leandro Maury Pentón were wounded in Magua, Trinidad, Sancti Spíritus. The bandits Ramón del Sol, Juan Guillermo Torres Fundora and Benito Rodríguez Lugones were involved in the event.

04/02/62　Combatant killed

Gusberto Guerra Hernández's band killed the combatant Ascanio Díaz Tamayo, at La Estrella neighborhood, Hermanos Mayo borough, Las Tunas.

04/04/62　Freelance killed

The taxi driver Pastor Rodríguez was kidnapped and killed at Zequeira rural estate, in Carlos Rojas, Matanzas.

04/16/62　Campesino killed

Rigoberto Tartabull Chacón's band killed Emeregildo Rodríguez Salas, in Charco Azul, Trinidad.

04/18/62　Campesinos killed

Benjamín "Pangüín" Tardío Hernández's band killed Camilo Fernández Toledo and his son Orestes at El Lomar rural estate, Aguacate neighborhood, Trinidad.

05/05/62　Campesino killed

Campesino Luis López Reyes and the thirteen-year-old boy Fermín Estévez Rodríguez, both neighbors of Retiro rural estate, Coliseo, Guamacaro, Matanzas, were kidnapped. Luis López Reyes was hanged and his body found by a batallion of Fight against Banditry (LCB) in the hills of La Esmeralda rural estate, Luis Salgado Cooperative, Coliseo, on 05/29/62. The boy was released. Idmelio "El Carnicero"[1] Rivera Chile's band committed this crime.

05/08/62　Militiamen killed

Raúl "Monono" Ramos Ramos' band assaulted the Pedro Morejón farm, in Monte Alto, Los Arabos, Matanzas, and killed the militiaman Jesús Mondéjar Chávez there.

05/11/62　Campeisnos wounded

Blas Tardío Hernández and Blas Ortega Ortega's band assaulted Francisco Hernández Domínguez's house and wound-

---

1. This nickname means "butcher." *Ed.*

ded Guillermo Hernández Niebla, his mother Adela Niebla Santos, René Hernández Niebla and Bertila Hernández Niebla, Francisco's children, in Cabaiguán.

05/19/62 COMBATANTS KILLED AND PERSON WOUNDED

Osmín Gorrín Vega's band killed the police sargeant Rómulo Padrón Díaz and severely wounded the militiaman Justo Pérez Michelena at Escaleras de Jaruco, La Habana. A few days later, the militiaman Agapito González Montanaro is killed in San Antonio de las Vegas.

05/22/62 CAMPESINOS KILLED

Valeriano "Vale" Montenegro Rodríguez's band killed Salvador Herrera Sarmientos, Aurelio E. Castillo Arbelo and Julio Martínez Leyva, at Jibacoa rural estate. Rodas, Cienfuegos.

05/25/62 CAMPESINOS WOUNDED

Gervasio Cabrera Hernández's band attacked the sugar-mill settlement, at El Caney rural estate, Pepe Prieto Cooperative, Dos Hermanos neighborhood, Calimete, Matanzas, and wounded Roberto and Rolando Elías Paz.

05/27/62 CAMPESINO KILLED

Ciro Vera Catalá's band killed Emilio Obregón Sirio, in Pelayo area, Jatibonico, Sancti Spíritus.

06/01/62 COMBATANT KILLED

Members of Delio Almeida's band killed Ramón Sánchez Estrada, responsible of the Public Order at the Rubén Martínez Villena farm, Amarillas neighborhood, Calimete, Matanzas.

06/03/62 CITIZEN WOUNDED

The citizen Jesús Yiloraméndez was wounded when part of Pedro Sánchez González's band attacked Jesús de Nazareno rural estate, in Agramonte, Matanzas.

06/13/62 MAN KILLED AND GIRL WOUNDED

Pedro Sánchez González's band shot a car and killed the driver, Domingo García Soto, and wounded the twelve-year-old girl Adela González Reyes and Amado González Espinosa, at Santa Ana rural estate, Gallardo neighborhood, Jagüey Grande, Matanzas.

06/15/62 CAMPESINOS KILLED

The militiamen campesinos Regino Padrón Giralde, Santiago Medina López and Orestes Hernández Rodríguez were kidnapped and subsequently killed in Seibabo, Yaguajay.

The bandits Arnoldo Martínez Andrade and Mario Bravo Cervantes were involved in the events.

06/16/62   MILITIAMAN KILLED AND MAN WOUNDED

Gabriel de Jesús Infante Hidalgo's band killed the militiaman Antonio Alemán Santana and wounded Severo Alemán in the area of the former Bellocino sugar-mill, Gildo Fleitas farm, Unión de Reyes, Matanzas.

06/17/62   CAMPESINO KILLED

Ramón del Sol Sorí's band killed the campesino Rafael Saroza Benítez Martínez, at Limones Cantero rural estate, Trinidad.

06/29/62   MILITIAMEN KILLED

Manuel "El Loco"[2] López López's band killed the militiamen Arbalio Molina Sánchez (20 years old) and Adalberto Sifontes Jiménez (18 years old) when the bus No. 18, where they were traveling from Chambas to Morón, Ciego de Ávila, was attacked.

07/02/62   CAMPESINOS KILLED

The band, under the command of Julio Emilio Carretero Escajadillo, killed the campesinos José Pío Romero, Ana Romero Rojas, and Eustaquio José Polo Romero at San José de Altamira rural estate, five kilometers from Condado, between Fomento and Trinidad, Sancti Spíritus. Also, the fourteen-year-old girl Paula Romero Rojas, her sister Teodora and her mother Vicenta Rojas were hit.

07/12/62   MILITIAMAN KILLED

Filiberto "El Pipero"[3] Coto Gómez's band killed the twenty-nine-year-old man Narciso Díaz "Chicho" Martínez, from Pinar del Río, member of the ORI, militiaman and agrarian leader, at Los Mangos. Osvaldo Sánchez, Güines, La Habana.

07/13/62   MILITIAMEN KILLED

Filiberto "El Pipero" Coto Gómez's band killed the sixty-two-year-old militiaman Porfirio Acosta Fernández, guard of El Manse rural estate, Ñico López Cooperative, Güines borough, La Habana.

07/15/62   MILITIAMAN KILLED

Oliverio Ibáñez Cadalzo headed an ambush where the militiaman Lucas Castellanos Rodríguez was killed in Loma de Cabagancito, Trinidad.

---

2. This nickname means "the madman." *Ed.*
3. This nickname means "the tanker driver." *Ed.*

07/16/62   COMBATANT KILLED

Porfirio Guillén Amador's band killed the combatant Manuel Bombino Guerra at San Isidro rural estate, Fomento, Sancti Spíritus.

07/24/62   CAMPESINO KILLED

Members of Porfirio Guillén Amador's band hanged Luis Cancio Castellanos in the La Ceiba Cooperative, Sancti Spíritus borough.

07/26/62   MILITIAMAN KILLED

Filiberto "El Pipero" Coto Gómez's band killed the thirty-six-year-old militiaman Humberto Fernández Piloto, chief of La Esperanza campesino-camp, at Armenteros rural estate, Güines borough, La Habana.

08/04/62   CAMPESINO KILLED

Pedro "El Suicida"[4] González Sánchez's band killed José Ibáñez at San Pedro farm, Trinidad. His remains were never found.

08/24/62   CAMPESINO KILLED

Counterrevolutionary bandits in the area, under the command of Filiberto Lara Tirado and the bandit Juan Iglesias Vilches killed Leonel Pérez Cárdenas, at Dolores hamlet, Cumanayagua, Cienfuegos.

08/28/62   CAMPESINO KILLED

The young campesino Rigoberto Inés Guash died when a grenade—hidden by Juan Antonio Montes de Oca Rodríguez's band—exploded.

09/01/62   CAMPESINOS KILLED

The band of Tomás David Pérez Díaz—known as Tomás San Gil—kidnapped Bienvenido Pardillo Quintero, from Guasimal, José Luis Abreu Ruiz, from La Habana, Luis Ramírez Salvador, from Santa Clara and Rodrigo Quintero Castro, from Peralejo, who were members of the Commission of Topographic Studies. Their remains were found in a common grave of Mapos, La Sierpe.

09/10/62   CITIZEN KILLED

A bandit group, under the command of Virgilio Claro Basulto —known as Capitán el Indio—killed Inocencio Villalba Sánchez at La Melva patch, Baracoa, Guantánamo.

---

4. This nickname means "the madcap." *Ed.*

09/15/62   TWO CAMPESINO LEADERS AND A SCHOOL TEACHER KILLED

The band of Tomás David Pérez Díaz—known as Tomás San Gil—killed Romelio Cornelio Pérez and Juan Giraldo González Suárez, two ANAP leaders, and the school teacher Pedro Antonio "Tony" Rodríguez, in Las Llanadas, Meyer neighborhood, Trinidad.

09/18/62   TWO CAMPESINOS WOUNDED

A bandit group attacked and wounded two campesinos when they were in a cooperative in Yaguajay.

11/02/62   WORKER KILLED AND BARNS BURNED

Esteban "Estebita" Morera Acosta's band killed (burned alive) the forest worker Jesús Sardiñas Suárez, at Abel Santamaría farm, Laguna del Pesquero rural estate, Cocodrilo neighborhood, Aguada de Pasajeros.

11/05/62   CAMPESINOS KILLED

Alfredo Amarantes "Maro" Borges Rodríguez's band killed the campesinos Estanislao "Lao" Gutiérrez Fleites, and Santiago Amador de la Cruz Salabarría, in Camilio Cienfuegos Cooperative, Guasimal area, Río Abajo, Sancti Spíritus.

11/12/62   MILITIAMAN KILLED

Porfirio R. Guillén Amador's band killed the militiaman Emérito Suárez Suárez at Jíquima neighborhood, Fomento.

12/62   CAMPESINO KILLED

Cipriano Almeida's band killed Hugo Pérez Viciedo. His body was found some months later at La Guerrilla rural estate, Justo Sánchez neighborhood, Jatibonico.

12/62   CAMPESINO KILLED

Osirio Borges Rojas's band killed Celestino García in Sancti Spíritus.

12/05/62   WORKER KILLED AND PEOPLE WOUNDED

Eliecer Martínez Socorro's band killed Lázaro González Fagundo and wounded Zunilda Morejón Morejón and Israel García Luzbet, when the jeep of the ORI—in which they were traveling to Quemado Grande, in Jagüey Grande, Matanzas, for exhibiting a movie to campesinos—was shot.

12/08/62   MILITIAMAN KILLED AND MAN WOUNDED

Frutoso Luis Molina Padrón and Miner de la Torre Martínez's bands killed the militiaman Julio de la Trinidad Martínez Leyva and his house burned. Also was wounded Andrés Cabañas Rodríguez, worker of El Novillo rural estate, in the neighborhood of Rodas borough.

12/18/62   STUDENT WOUNDED

A group of bandits, belonging to Tomás San Gil's band, attacked train No. 42, Trinidad-Santa Clara, at Km 54 between Meyer and Manacal, Trinidad. The seventeen-year-old student Félix Corredera Delgado was wounded.

12/23/62   CAMPESINO KILLED AND MAN WOUNDED

Counterrevolutionary elements, under the command of ringleaders Pedro "El Suicida" González Sánchez, and José Tápanes Tápanes, killed the militiaman campesino Oliverio Marín Valdivia, and wounded his brother Riordano Marín Valdivia, from Arenal suburb, Casilda, Trinidad. These elements also burned the town's store.

12/28/62   FARM ADMINISTRATOR AND WORKER KILLED

Gilberto "Candela"[5] Vera Acosta's band killed the administrator of Patrice Lumumba farm, Flores Colina Díaz, the worker José Tristá. The killings took place at Nuevas neighborhood, Ranchuelo, Las Villas.

5. This nickname means "fire." *Ed.*

Espionage Networks Created by the U.S. Intelligence that Performed in Cuba during the Operation Mongoose

Case: Principio [Principle]
Date: Late 1959 – Mid 1963

Espionage network, whose main agent and the rest of its members belonged to the counterrevolutionary organization Revolutionary Democratic Action (ADR). The agent was trained in a U.S. base. He received radio transmissions from the CIA Main Station, and also used as liaison an employee of a European embassy within Cuba. The agent infiltrated through maritime via in three occasions for carrying out tasks of military espionage.

Case: Reina [Queen] Date:
Late 1959 – October 1964

Espionage network directed by the CIA; its main agent was originally from Santiago de Cuba, Cuban citizen, and professor of Geography at the Havana Institute, who was recruited in August 1962. His recruiting officer was the main agent of the network and, subsequently, when leaving the country, he received intelligence abroad. Some members and collaborators were former military officers of the tyranny. They developed activities of military and scientific espionage. Also they should inform the economic operations concerning entrance and sorties of ships and merchandise they brought. This network consisted in three agents and twenty-two collaborators.

Case: Abandono [Abandonment]
Date: 1959 – February 1965

The main agent of this espionage network directed by the CIA was originally from Spain, Cuban citizen, translator, and was recruited by the

U.S. embassy in Havana. In this case, it was learned the existence of two espionage networks, one in Camagüey Province, and the other one in La Habana. In the latter, there were four agents who were in direct contact with the CIA. The general tasks given to the agents were military, economic, and scientific espionage. Approximately twenty-six collaborators were involved in these tasks.

Case: Arrepentido [Regretted]
Date: December 1960 – 1963
Espionage network directed by the CIA. Its main agent was originally from Ciego de Ávila. He was recruited outside of Cuba in 1960. He returned legally to Cuba in early 1961. He recruited fifteen collaborators. Their espionage task was taking pictures of areas to carry out aerial droppings of weapons.

Case: Moto-Tabaco [Moto-Tobacco]
Date: Late 1960 – Early 1966
The main agent of this espionage network was employed in the Purchase Section, Supply Department, Ministry of Transport. The main role of this espionage network, created by the U.S. embassy in our country before its departure, was to obtain intelligence regarding transport and reporting on movements of military convoys and Soviet troops inside of Cuba. The network activity comprised Pinar del Río and La Habana provinces. It had twenty-four members.

Case: Largo-Chancleta [Long-slipper]
Date: 1961 – December 1963
Espionage network, with some fifteen collaborators, whose main agent was originally from Pinar del Río. The main task of this network was to obtain intelligence, even though initially the main mission to fulfill had been trying to contribute to armed uprising. By late 1962, when operating the Cura case it was checked that the agent sent intelligence to the CIA Station through a European embassy.

Case: Cura-Manco [Priest-One-handed Man]
Date: 1961 – February 1965
The main agent of this CIA espionage network had been a public official and politician during the tyranny. Landowner, he was recruited by a CIA agent infiltrated in our country in 1961. He was trained through mail, by means of the diplomatic baggage of a European embassy. He held technical means to contact the CIA. The main task of this network

137

consisted in obtaining military, political, and economic intelligence, although he had an outstanding involvement in the execution of the Operation Peter Pan. Several figures of the bourgeoisie belonged to this network. Twelve agents of the network had direct contact with the CIA and it comprised more than sixty-five collaborators. This network was entrusted in carrying out a plot to assassinate the Commander in Chief Fidel Castro Ruz. To do so, he planned to use a counterrevolutionary element, who worked at Habana Libre Hotel, who should poison the Chief of the Revolution when he was to have a shake in the cafeteria of the hotel.

Case: 2949
Date: January 1961 – April 1961
The main agent of this espionage network was originally from Santiago de Cuba. Trade dealer. He was one of the chiefs of the MRR. This network had ten members and obtained intelligence of political and economic interest in Oriente Province.

Case: Río Verde [Green River]
Date: February 1961 – April 1961
Espionage network, whose main agent was originally from La Habana. Student on architecture, anti-Communist element, militant of the counterrevolutionary organization MRR. His main task was to obtain military intelligence and recruit individuals amongst military men.

Case: Solución [Solution]
Date: February 1961 – January 1965
The main agent of this espionage network was candidate to representative during the period of Batista's dictatorship. He migrated to the United States in June 1960, where he was recruited. He returned to Cuba in 1962. The network comprised four collaborators, trained by the CIA. Missions of this network comprised obtaining military intelligence and possible winning of active service men of armed institutions.

Case: Presidencial [Presidential]
Date: April 1961 – June 1963
Espionage network, which had a main agent, originally from La Habana. Public Accountant. At the moment of the triumph of the Revolution he was working in the banking sector. He was ringleader of the

counterrevolutionary organization M-30-11 and the MRR. This espionage network was devoted to seek military, economic and political intelligence. Seventeen collaborators made up this network.

Case: Fiera [Savage]
Date: May 1961 – October 1963
During the tyranny, the main agent of this espionage network belonged to the Authentic Organization (OA), and was friend of the former President Carlos Prío Socarrás. He was recruited in the United States by Orlando Puente, former Carlos Prío Socarrás' secretary and CIA agent, who trained him in a hotel in Miami, in May 1961. The agent confessed to have created a cell of informants, well compartmentalized, which sent some 200 messages to the enemy for 2 years.

Case: Petróleo [Oil]
Date: September 1961 – March 1965
Espionage network in which its main agent, when finishing his higher studies of mechanic engineering at Louisiana University in the United States, was recruited by the CIA to carry out espionage activities in Cuba in the early days of February 1962. When arriving in Cuba, he started to work at the Petroleum Enterprise where he began to develop his espionage activity, transferring the CIA intelligence regarding such an enterprise and carrying out instructions received from its station in Miami. Subsequently, the main activity consisted in studying conditions in order to execute a plan of sabotage at the Ñico López Refinery, so he began to recruit four collaborators. In 1964, the CIA Station assigned him the task to carry out sabotage in crude oil pipelines and tanks, and therefore, to paralyze the refinery through a sabotage act. This action was frustrated.

Case: Pizza
Date: September 1961 – April 1966
The main agent of this espionage network was originally from Spain. He was a official at Havana Customs. The CIA recruited him in Miami on September 5, 1961. This network gave economic, political and military intelligence. It had two collaborators.

Case: Carlitos-Menudo [Carlitos-Tiny]
Date: October 1961 – January 1962
Espionage network directed by the CIA. Its main agent was originally from La Habana, former member of the tyrant Batista's police. He

had close relations with the nephews of the henchman Salas Cañizares. He traveled to the United States in September 1961. He was recruited by a CIA agent in August or September 1961. This network was created and divided into two cells for obtaining military, political, and economic intelligence. This network had nine collaborators, all of them former members of Batista's army and members of different counterrevolutionary organizations, such as Anti-Communist Patriotic Action Movement and M-30-11.

Case: Patilla [Sideburn]
Date: October 1961 – July 1963
The main agent of this espionage network, before the triumph of the Revolution, was in the United States and belonged to its army. He was recruited by the CIA in 1961. The mission of this espionage network of nine members, directed by the CIA, was the recruiting of counterrevolutionary elements among the organizations MRR, MRP and M-30-11, in order to obtain military intelligence and that concerning the entrance and departure of Soviet ships, among other tasks.

Case: Astuto [Astute]
Date: December 1961 – March 1964
The main agent of this espionage network was originally from Camagüey. This network was made up of elements of the bourgeoisie belonging to the Havana Lions Club, and had some agents trained by the CIA. The agent started working as CIA agent when coming back from the United States on January 13, 1962, with the mission to obtain intelligence of political interest and to make contacts with other agents. In April of the same year, the agent was back to Miami, coming back to Cuba on January 6, 1963, with instructions to recruit people with access to military bases, or figures of the Revolutionary Government. Obtained intelligence was sent to the center through mailboxes, receiving instructions directly. This network had collaborators in Camagüey, Las Villas, La Habana and Oriente.

Case: Abantes (5235)
Date: Late 1961 – November 1962
The main agent of this espionage network was originally from Las Villas. He belonged to Batista's army with official ranks. He left the country in May 1959 in a boat, by violent means, together with other counterrevolutionary elements, amongst them, the one who subsequently

140

is recruited by the CIA as instructor of mercenaries, of Cuban origin, who trained for the invasion. He was the Chief of the commands of the Group of Special Missions (GME) in the CIA operational unit in Florida, known as JM-WAVE. The agents, whom he infiltrated with, received training by the CIA to carry out the blowing of a mine at Matahambre, in Pinar del Río. This action was frustrated with the arrest of the infiltration team.

Case: 220-Oriente
Date: Late ·1961 – May 1964

Espionage network; its main agent was originally from Santiago de Cuba. He worked at the Planning and Statistics Department of the Ministry of Domestic Trade (MINCIN) in Oriente. He was recruited to belong to a counterrevolutionary organization (MRR) giving him different tasks, such as espionage activity, which he undertook through the Naval Base of Guantánamo. This espionage network was made up of active elements of the counterrevolutionary organization MRR and its main task was to obtain intelligence of economic, political and military character. Economic intelligence regarding existing supplies in Oriente Province and its distributing network was very important.

Case: Mago (Cogñac) [Magician (Cogñac)]
Date: Late 1961 – December 1964

The main agent of this CIA espionage network was originally from Yaguajay, Villa Clara. This network was made up of people living in Pinar del Río, La Habana, Matanzas, and Villa Clara provinces, who carried out espionage using the diplomatic baggage of a European embassy to sent intelligence to the CIA. This network had twenty-six collaborators.

Case: Yanqui [Yankee]
Date: Late 1961 – May 1965

CIA espionage network with fifteen collaborators. Its main agent was originally from Stochbridge, Massachusetts, U.S.A., whose job was cattle raiser. He belonged to the U.S. Army and was involved in the Korean War. He settled down in Cuba as landowner, so was affected by the Agrarian Reform Act. He was recruited by the then Director of the CIA, Allen Dulles. This network gave intelligence of military and economic character in Pinar del Río Province.

141

Case: FUO
Date: 1962 – May 1964
  The main agent of this espionage network was originally from Pinar del Río Province. He upraised in 1960 and when annihilating the band, he took asylum in the Argentinean embassy. He was recruited by the CIA in Venezuela and infiltrated in our country in March 1962. Then, he began the creation of the network, recruiting his relatives. Twelve main agents operated in the network. Candidates to be recruited were proposed to collaborate for a counterrevolutionary organization, although activity was directly with the CIA. Between February and March 1962, the network was active in the sending of military intelligence, task that achieves the highest significance during the Cuban Missile Crisis. In December 1963, the network split into eight commands through a territorial division: four in Pinar del Río, three in La Habana, and one in Isle of Pines. This network played an outstanding role for the enemy in plans of Operation Mongoose in 1962.

Case: Malecón
Date: 1962 – September 1964
  Espionage network under the direction of the CIA, whose main agent submitted military intelligence to the CIA.

Case: Nacional [National]
Date: 1962 – October 1964
  Espionage network under the direction of the CIA, with a main agent, who was originally from Camagüey. He was recruited by his brother, who took asylum at the Naval Base of Guantánamo. In this case, two networks were operated, in which there were contacts with another network that operated in La Habana Province. The task of this network was to provide political, military, and economic intelligence. The CIA requested intelligence regarding Camagüey airport and units of Soviet troops in the province.

Case: Ola [Wave]
Date: 1962 – March 1965
  The main agent of this CIA espionage network was trained in Cuba. He had close relations with a CIA female agent. His missions were aimed at seeking intelligence regarding missile bases and their positions, other interesting data on the Armed Forces, particularly the Revolutionary Navy, the arrival of merchant ships in the country, railroad movements in the national territory, amongst other interests.

142

Case: Pormirón
Date: Half 1962 – March 1968
Its main agent was agronomic engineer and sugar-chemical expert. He studied Chemistry Engineer in Tulane, Louisiana University, United States, between 1936 and 1939. He owned a sugar plantation. He recruited fifteen collaborators, taking advantage of his friendly relations with these people. He was trained in our country; the CIA supplied an RR-48-A plant, with instructions for its manipulation, and deciphering pad kits. The main tasks received by the agent were sending intelligence of economic, political, and military character, particularly sugar industry and the Soviet military staff in the country. During his illegal activity, he transferred some 240 messages to the CIA.

Case: Operación Santa Clara-Luna-Escorpión
[Operation Santa Clara-Moon-Scorpion]
Date: March 1962 – January 1964
The principal agent of this espionage network under the direction of the CIA was originally from Santa Clara, whose job was accountancy. The mission of the network was to obtain military, economic, and political intelligence, as well as to sabotage the economy, and it had sixty-five collaborators. Amongst its missions, it was also entrusted in receiving agents and infiltration teams from the United States, for picking up intelligence, being a liaison, or supplying bandit groups with equipments and weapons at the Escambray. The CIA had instructed the network not to make contact with counterrevolutionary organizations for preventing from being found out. During its activity, the command of the network held close links of intelligence with authorities of a European embassy.

Case: Gato Negro [Black Cat] or Espías [Spies]
Date: June 1962 – December 1962
The main agent of this espionage network, under the direction of the CIA, was opposed to the Revolution, because he was affected by revolutionary laws. He penetrated in the Naval Base of Guantánamo after the victory of Playa Girón. The CIA recruited him at Coral Gables, Florida, in early 1962. In Cuba, he organizes a broad network in mountainous areas in the vicinity of Guantánamo and Santiago de Cuba, sending intelligence to the CIA Station on political and economic situation. The main activity of the agents was military espionage, carried out until December 20, 1962. According to instructions received by the U.S. intelligence agencies, his plans should focus to organizing

143

three guerrilla fronts in Oriente mountains, since the landing of small amounts of weapons, in certain places of the southern coast of Oriente, was already foreseen.

Case: Anillo [Ring]
Date: Mid 1962 – September 1965
The main agent of this espionage network under the direction of the CIA was originally from Pinar del Río. He was ringleader of the organization Revolutionary Unity, in which held the post of Military Coordinator of Pinar del Río Province. He was recruited by the CIA for the also agent known as Larry, mid 1962. When the agent starts to organize his espionage network, he thought of the same elements that he already knew from his conspiracy activities. The network had thirty-four collaborators in Pinar del Río, twenty-three in La Habana, and three in Matanzas. Intelligence to be sent to CIA station was economic and military. In March 1965, the CIA Station instructs him to establish possible places for exfiltration, which were to be used for illegally taking out other conspirators of the country.

Case: Tejano [Texan]
Date: Mid 1962 – November 1965
Espionage network under the direction of the CIA, whose main agent was originally from Camagüey. Before the triumph of the Revolution he had close relations with elements of the tyranny. This network also had another agent. The CIA trained them in secret writing, in early 1963. They provided intelligence concerning the different troop mobilizations in our territory, location of our bases and military camps, and political and economic intelligence requested through the subversive radio station The Voice of the Americas.

Case: Piano
Date: July 1962 – September 1963
Espionage network, under the direction of the CIA, whose main agent was recruited in July 1962 and trained in secret writing. One of the main tasks was to obtain intelligence regarding military units of the Revolutionary Armed Forces (FAR), as well as intelligence of economic character, showing interest in existing ships at port, their cargoes, and countries. These intelligence data were obtained through visual observation or in talks with workers of those places, transmitting these between July 1962 and August 1963, by international mail.

Case: Popeye
Date: July 1962 – July 1965

Espionage network under the direction of the CIA, whose main agent was originally from Guantánamo. He belonged to the Cuban merchant fleet. A CIA agent, booked at Tres Cepas Hotel recruited him, when arriving as crewmember of the ship *Aracelio Iglesias* to Valencia, Spain. This agent should make report on Cuba, mainly about loading and unloading, merchandises, and on crew members of the Cuban merchant ships, using his collaborators as courier for introducing subversive material and communication means in Cuba for supplying other intelligence networks. Another task assigned to him was the choosing of some Cuban crewmembers to have interviews with CIA agents in foreign ports.

Case: Corresponsal [Correspondent]
Date: August 1962 – June 1963

Espionage network under the CIA conduction, whose main agent traveled to the United States in 1961, where he was recruited. The recruited agents as informants sent economic, political, and military intelligence, and press clippings obtained from the public press, by the correspondence. Specific tasks of these informants were received through Luis Conte Agüero's radio program in the radio station The Voice of the Americas. In their activities of openly obtaining intelligence, other persons opposed to the Revolution assisted them. A lot of intelligence was thus obtained: snooping around main roads, and in occasions, following military caravans.

Case: Niágara [Niagara]
Date: September 1962 – September 1965

Espionage network under the direction of the CIA, where its main agent was originally from Güira de Melena, La Habana. He illegally left the national territory on August 14, 1962. Once in the U.S. territory, he was recruited a month later for military service, being transferred to Fort Knox, Kentucky. And a month after being detached in such a camp, he was transferred to Fort Jackson, South Carolina, where he completed the six-month training Cuban immigrants usually took at the time. While living in Miami, he entered the counterrevolutionary organization Christian Democratic Movement, and then in another group called Free Commands. In September 1965, the CIA infiltrated the agent in Cuba to open an espionage network in the area of Romano Cay, in the northern coast of Camagüey.

Case: Operación K [Operation K]
Date: October 1962 – March 1963

Espionage network under the direction of the CIA, whose main agent illegally migrated to the United States in August 1961. He was recruited in December and trained by the CIA in a security house located in the road between Miami and Key West and in a military base. This network was made up of other two agents. This infiltration team penetrates in the country on October 1, 1962 through Caharatas Beach. According to statements of the agent, they had two specific missions to fulfill: to open a maritime reception cell to introduce weapons and to try to locate the bases for Soviet missiles and to report on the Soviet bases of the northern coast. On December 11, 1962 he was captured.

Case: Internacional [International]
Date: November 1962 – May 1965

Espionage network under the direction of the CIA, whose main agent was originally from La Habana. Lawyer and judicial technical advisor of the Cuban Aviation Company. The agent is recruited and, at the same time, is the one who carries out recruitment of other collaborators and informants. He was trained the three times he traveled abroad from 1962 onwards. The first training is undertaken in the outskirts of Switzerland in September 1962. The second training at Bernabeu Stadium, Madrid, Spain, in September 1963. The last one in the Torre de Madrid building, at Spain Plaza, Madrid, September 1964. His general training consisted in secret writing from September 1962 to September 1963, both for receiving and transmitting intelligence.

Case: Retorno [Return]
Date: December 1962 – Mid 1964

Espionage network under the direction of the CIA, whose main agent was originally from La Habana. He lived in the United States in the 1940-46 period. He belonged to the army of that country being given the rank of Captain. He was involved in the World War II. Upon his return in Cuba, he was appointed agent of the Bureau of Investigation during the administration of the former President Ramón Grau San Martín, for recommendations of his friend Emilio Tro; he stayed in that repressive Corps until 1951. In February 1958 he began working in the former Havana Hilton Hotel as Assistance of the Security Chief. In late October 1958 he moved to Sierra del Escambray, where he remained until January 1, 1959 as combatant of the Revolutionary Directorate March 13.

Upon his return, he was appointed Captain of the Revolutionary Navy, up to the moment when committing betrayal act and illegally he left the country in a small plane he used for his responsibilities. In the United States the CIA recruited him to fulfill multiple subversive tasks on Cuba. The CIA headquarters was interested that he would deal with individuals who could make sabotage in planes. On September 4, 1965 he was captured when trying to infiltrate in the national territory through Varadero Beach.

Case: Transmisor [Transmitter]
Date: Late 1962 – January 1965
Espionage network under the direction of the CIA, whose main agent was member of the counterrevolutionary organizations The White Rose, M-30-11, Democratic National Front (FND), and Revolutionary Unity. He was recruited to organize a receptionist network in May, or June 1963 by a CIA agent, newly infiltrated. Once he was recruited, he was given the task to recruit other elements to integrate such a network, which came to have thirty-two collaborators. This network was captured when its members were operating in the northern coast of Las Villas; it undertook different weapons, equipments and explosives deposits, landed by other CIA agents.

Case: Gamo [Fallow deer]
Date: March 1963 – March 1966
Espionage network under the direction of the CIA. Its main agent was originally from Guantánamo, His recruitment took place when he started his conspiracy activities in April 1959, making contact with the former military man of the tyranny, Horacio Morales, from the Naval Base. He carried out different conspiracy activities such as introducing weapons and plans of uprisings, by which he was in prison in 1961. During his training as agent, he received mail-instruction to make messages in secret writing, or revealing and writing in "carbon" paper. Between March 1963 and March 1966 this network transferred its intelligence to elements residing at the Naval Base and in Miami City, who, at the same time, sent them to the Naval Intelligence Service and the CIA.

Case: Suspenso [Suspense]
Date: March 1963 – July 1965
Espionage network under the direction of the CIA. Its main agent studied in the United States. Former landowner, with some 2805 acres

of land, one of his sons was involved in Bay of Pigs invasion. This citizen had relations with former representatives of the tyranny. A CIA official recruited him on November 15, 1962, when traveling to the United States. He was trained in a house located south Miami. He received general training on organization of clandestine networks, recruitment, counterchecking, secret writing, phonics reception, maps reading, signals with infra-red paper, and micro-point techniques. His tasks were to submit political, military, and economic intelligence of Manzanillo area (fulfilled). This espionage network had some twenty-two collaborators.

Case: Piloto [Pilot]
Date: May 1963
Espionage network under the direction of the CIA, whose main agent was former lieutenant of Batista's army. Plans of the CIA were fostering espionage networks in Oriente Province for obtaining military and economic intelligence. As main agent, he was entrusted of recruiting and training supporting agents who later commanded as Chief of network from the Naval Base of Guantánamo, using personal contact as communication and linking means, with more than twenty collaborators.

Case: Pionero [Pioneer]
Date: May 1963 – 1964
Espionage network under the direction of the CIA, whose main agent was ringleader of the counterrevolutionary organizations Revolutionary Unit and Rescue. He was clandestinely sent to the United States in August 1962. Recruited and trained by the CIA in Miami, he was subsequently transferred to Panama where he takes a course on explosive matter. Back to Miami, he was trained in intelligence techniques, secret writing, checking, and counterchecking. In May 1963 he infiltrated as part of a CIA team for preparing sabotage to the Telephone Enterprise, Electricity Enterprise (Tallapiedra and Regla), and oil refineries in Oriente and La Habana, and on the transport sector. Before this travel, the group had other two attempts of infiltration, one during the Cuban Missile Crisis and the other in April 1963. Its intention was to obtain all possible intelligence regarding presumed missile bases in Isabela de Sagua and San Julián, and organizing an espionage network in Matanzas.

148

Case: Agentes de Cayo Verde [Agents of Verde Cay]
Date: July 1963

Espionage network under the direction of the CIA, whose main agent was originally from Isabela de Sagua, Las Villas. He illegally left the country on January 25, 1961, where was recruited by the CIA. The network had other two agents. The first infiltration of this group in Cuba took place on June 14, 1963, in a key of the Sagua area, occasion when a platform, made of plywood, was built, which could be used to keep materiel, or hiding a person. In the second occasion, they reached to Verde Cay, where they were arrested.

Case: Esperando [Awaiting]
Date: July 1963 – April 1964

Espionage network under the direction of the CIA, whose main agent was originally from Puerto Padre, Oriente. He conspired in the counter-revolutionary organization Christian Democratic Movement and left the country. He was trained in the Trax Base in Guatemala for the Bay of Pigs invasion. He took military classes at the Everglades (swampy area in Florida). He received training in secret writing for communications. He was arrested with other agents when tried to infiltrate into the country.

Case: Dima
Date: July 1963 – August 1967

Network under the direction of the CIA, with main agent originally from Los Palacios, Pinar del Río; former politicaster and with close relations with the former President Carlos Prío Socarrás. On June 11, 1961, he illegally leaves the country through Punta Colorada, Pinar del Río. Recruited in 1965 by a CIA agent, he was trained in the United States, where he received intelligence preparation. According to statements of a group of agents he trained with, this group was involved in infiltration operations, all through the northern coast of Pinar del Río. before being arrested.

Case: Claxon
Date: September 1963

Espionage network under the direction of the CIA, its agent was recruited and trained in the United States. This agent illegally penetrated into the country through maritime via in four occasions, in order to recruit elements, give them weapons and fight the Revolution. The last time he infiltrated, in September 1963, he did so through Las Villas Province, in a speedboat from Miami. He had the mission to organize a military espionage network, as well as to introduce weapons and receive other agents aimed at providing the necessary support for invasion.

Case: La Empalizada [The Palisade]
Date: September 1963
Espionage network under the direction of the CIA, whose main agent was an employee at the air company Aerovías Q. He left Cuba via Mexico on September 1, 1962, prior taking asylum at Uruguay embassy, and traveled from Mexico to Miami, where he was recruited. This network was made up of other agents and was aimed at obtaining military photographs on kinds of weapons and military emplacements. They were captured on September 10, 1963.

Case: Occidente [West]
Date: April 1963 – October 1963
Espionage network under the direction of the CIA, its main agent was originally from La Habana. He owned boats. He illegally left the country on August 20, 1961 bound for the United States where the CIA recruited him. The general tasks received by this group of agents were infiltration through Pinar del Río Province in order to create networks to provide military, political and economic intelligence. This network had seven main agents and more than forty-two collaborators.

Case: Metascope
Date: August 1963 – November 1963
Espionage network under the direction of the CIA, whose agent was customs broker and Public Works contractor. He left the country, to reside in Miami onwards. He was recruited in December 1960 and was trained in two Inns near Miami airport. He should check, within our country, all intelligence that the Pentagon received from a spy. The CIA instructed him to create an intelligence network that got to have more than fifteen collaborators.

Case: Pinar del Río
Date: December 1963 – January 1965
Espionage network under the direction of the CIA, whose main agent was originally from Pinar del Río. After the triumph of the Revolution, he clandestinely left the country in June 1962. On December 5, 1963 he

was recruited by the CIA through the counterrevolutionary organization MRR, using this terrorist organization as a cover. The two agents of this network were trained in a camp located in rainforests of Costa Rica, in a place known as Sarapigui. The task of this espionage network in our country was to fulfill the CIA so-called mission Operation Wolf, consisting in infiltrating through the southern coast of Pinar del Río (blindly) and studying the area in order to seek a safe place for infiltrating other groups. These agents infiltrated in Cuba on December 29, 1964, from the Zenón base, Nicaragua, on board of *Santa Lucía* ship, under the custody of two boats armed with two machine-guns caliber 50, which brought them up to Guamá river-mouth, where they board a rubber-raft downstream up to terra firma. There they were subsequently arrested.

BIBLIOGRAPHY

BOOKS, ARTICLES AND DOCUMENTS

ARBOLEYA CERVERA, JESÚS. *The Cuban Counterrevolution*. Havana: Editorial José Martí, 2002.

ARIET GARCÍA, MARÍA DEL CARMEN. "El Pensamiento Político de Ernesto Che Guevara" [The Political Thought of Ernesto Che Guevara]. Ph.D. diss., University of Havana, 1987.

BURKHOLDER SMITH, JOSEPH. *Retrato de un guerrero frío* [Portrait of a Cold Warrior]. Havana: Editorial Capitán San Luis, 1993.

CASTRO RUZ, FIDEL. *History Will Absolve Me*. Annotated Edition. Havana: Editorial José Martí, 1998.

_____. *Discursos* [Speeches], Vol 1. Havana: Editorial de Ciencias Sociales, 1975.

CHANG, LAURENCE and PETER KORNBLUH, ED. *The Cuban Missile Crisis, 1962: A National Security Archive Documents Reader*. New York: New Press, 1992.

CHARISIUS, ALBRECHT and JULIUS MADER. *Nicht Länger Geheim*. Berlin: Deutscher Militärverlag, 1969.

COLBY, WILLIAM and PETER FORBATH. *Honorable Man. My Life in the CIA*. New York: Simon & Schuster, 1978.

COLLECTIVE WORK. *Historia de Cuba 1930-1959* [Cuban History, 1930-59]. Havana: Editorial Pueblo y Educación, 1985.

COMISIÓN DE HISTORIA DE LOS ÓRGANOS DE LA SEGURIDAD DEL ESTADO. *Historia de la Seguridad Cubana* [History of the Cuban Security Bodies]. Havana: Ministry of the Interior, 1988.

CIHSE. Relación de investigaciones sobre planes de atentados en los años 1961-1962 [List of Investigations on Plots of Assassinations in 1961-62]. Havana, 1994.

CORN, DAVID. *Blond Ghost: Ted Shackley and the CIA Crusades*. New York: Simon & Schuster, 1994.

Cuadernos de Estudios, No. 1, 2 and 3. Havana, 1994-1995.

DIDION, JOAN. *Miami*. New York: Pocket Books, 1988.

ESCALANTE FONT, FABIÁN. *Cuba: La Guerra secreta de la CIA contra Cuba* [Cuba: The Secret War on Cuba]. Havana: Editorial Capitán San Luis, 1993.

_____. "Estados Unidos frente a la Revolución Cubana. El Proyecto Cuba" [The United States before the Cuban Revolution. The Cuba Project]. Research report. Ministry of the Interior, Havana, 1994.

ETCHEVERRY VÁZQUEZ, PEDRO. "La Guerra irregular de la CIA en la Operación Mangosta" [The Guerrilla Warfare of CIA in the Operation Mongoose]. Research report. CIHSE, Havana, 2002.

FONER, PHILLIP. *A History of Cuba and Its Relations with the United States*. Vol 1, *1492-1845 From the Conquest of Cuba to La Escalera*. New York: International Publishers, 1962. .

GARCÍA ITURBE, NÉSTOR. "La política de Estados Unidos hacia Cuba. De Ford a Clinton" [The United States Policy towards Cuba. From Ford to Clinton]. Ph.D. diss., University of Havana, 1997.

HEINRICH, EBERHARD and KLAUS ULRICH. *Der Krieg einer unsichtbaren Armee. Porträt der CIA*. Berlin: Militärverlag der Deutschen Demokratischen Republik, 1983.

HERNÁNDEZ MARTÍNEZ, JORGE. "Seguridad Nacional y Política Latinoamericana de Estados Unidos: la dimensión ideológica" [National Security and the United States Latin American Policy: The Ideological Dimension]. Ph.D. diss., University of Havana, 1998.

HERSH, SEYMOUR. *The Dark Side of Camelot*. Boston: Little, Brown & Company, 1997.

HINCKLE, WARREN and WILLIAM TURNER. *The Fish is Red: The Story of the Secret War against Castro*. New York: Harper and Row Publisher, 1981.

HUBERMAN, LEO and PAUL SWEEZY. *Socialism in Cuba*. N.p.: Monthly Review Press, 1969.

JARAMILLO EDWARDS, ISABEL. "El conflicto de baja intensidad. Modelo para armar" [Conflict of Low Intensity: Model to Assemble]. *Avances de investigación,* no. 24 (Havana: 1989).

KENNEDY, ROBERT. *Robert Kennedy ante el Congreso: Polémica* [Robert Kennedy before the Congress]. Havana: Instituto Cubano del Libro, 1968.

_____. *Thirteen days. A Memoir of the Cuban Missile Crisis.* New York: W. W. Norton and Company, Inc., 1969.

LÓPEZ SEGRERA, FRANCISCO et al. *De Eisenhower a Reagan* [From Eisenhower to Reagan]. Havana: Editorial de Ciencias Sociales, 1987.

MARCHETTI, VICTOR and JOHN MARKS. *The CIA and Cult of Intelligence.* New York: Dell Publishing Co. Inc., 1974.

MATTHEWS, HERBERT. "Regreso a Cuba" [Back to Cuba]. Typewritten translation in the CIHSE Archives, 1963.

MÉNDEZ MÉNDEZ, JOSÉ LUIS. "Terrorismo de origen cubano, 1959-1996 [Terrorism of Cuban Origin. 1959-1996]. Ph.D. diss., University of Havana, 1997.

MINISTRY OF THE ARMED FORCES. Informe Especial del Estado Mayor General de las FAR [Special Report of the General Chief of Staff, Revolutionary Armed Forces. Havana, January 19, 1963.

MINISTRY OF THE INTERIOR. Informe Especial sobre planes del Imperialismo contra la Revolución Cubana [Special Report on Plans of Imperialism against the Cuban Revolution]. Havana, June 21, 1962.

_____. Informe sobre el impacto de la Operación Mangosta en Camagüey [Report on Impact of Operation Mongoose in Camagüey]. Havana, 2002.

_____. Informe sobre el impacto de la Operación Mangosta en Ciego de Ávila [Report on Impact of Operation Mongoose in Ciego de Ávila]. Havana, 2002.

_____. Informe sobre el impacto de la Operación Mangosta en Cienfuegos [Report on Impact of Operation Mongoose in Cienfuegos]. Havana, 2002.

_____. Informe sobre el impacto de la Operación Mangosta en el Municipio Especial Isla de la Juventud [Report on Impact of Operation Mongoose in the Special Municipality of the Isle of Youth]. Havana, 2002.

_____. Informe sobre el impacto de la Operación Mangosta en Granma [Report on Impact of Operation Mongoose in Granma]. Havana, 2002.

_____. Informe sobre el impacto de la Operación Mangosta en Las Tunas [Report on Impact of Operation Mongoose in Las Tunas]. Havana, 2002.

_____. Informe sobre el impacto de la Operación Mangosta en Pinar del Río [Report on Impact of Operation Mongoose in Pinar del Río]. Havana, 2002.

_____. Informe sobre el impacto de la Operación Mangosta en Sancti Spíritus [Report on Impact of Operation Mongoose in Sancti Spíritus]. Havana, 2002.

_____. Informe sobre el impacto de la Operación Mangosta en Villa Clara [Report on Impact of Operation Mongoose in Villa Clara]. Havana, 2002.

_____. Informe sobre la actividad subversive enemiga en el período de la Operación Mangosta [Report on Enemy Subversive Activity in the Period of the Operation Mongoose]. Havana, 2002.

_____. Informe sobre la Operación AM/LASH [Report on the Operation AM/LASH]. Havana, 1997.

_____. Informe sobre las actividades desarrolladas por el agente de la CIA AM/LASH en el exterior [Report on Activities Developed by CIA Agent AM/LASH Abroad], Havana 1964-65.

_____. Informe sobre los grupos especiales de la CIA en el año 1963 [Report on Special Groups of CIA in 1963]. Havana, 1968.

_____. Informe [Report]. Paper presented at the Seminary on Ideological Diversionism, Havana, 1974.

_____. Records for Espionage Cases during 1961, 1962 and 1963 (57 cases).

PARTIDO COMUNISTA DE CUBA. *Informe al I Congreso del Partido Comunista de Cuba* [Report to the I Congress of the Cuban Communist Party]. Havana: Editorial Pueblo y Educación, 1978.

PATERSON, THOMAS G. *Contesting Castro*. Oxford: Oxford University Press, 1994.

PREVAILING WINDS RESEARCH, ED. *CIA Assassination Plots. A Report from the Inspector General on Plots to Assassinate Fidel Castro*. Introduction by Peter Dale Scott, Ph.D. N.p.: 1994.

Primera Conferencia de Solidaridad de los Pueblos de América Latina: Economía e Intervención [First Solidarity Conference of Latin American Peoples: Economy and Intervention]. Vol 3. Havana: Instituto Cubano del Libro, 1968.

POWERS, THOMAS. *The Man Who Kept the Secrets. Richard Helms and the CIA*. New York: Alfred A. Knopf, 1979.

RIVERO COLLADO, CARLOS. *Los sobrinos del tío Sam* [The Nephews of Uncle Sam]. Havana: Editorial de Ciencias Sociales, 1976.

RODRÍGUEZ, CARLOS RAFAEL. *Letra con filo* [Sharpened Letter]. Vol 2. Havana: Editorial de Ciencias Sociales, 1983.

RODRÍGUEZ, JUAN CARLOS. *La batalla inevitable* [The Inevitable Battle]. Havana: Editorial Capitán San Luis, 1996.

SCHEER, ROBERT and MAURICE ZEITLIN. *Cuba: An American Tragedy*. Great Britain: Penguin Books, 1964.

SCHLESINGER, ARTHUR JR. *A Thousand Days: John F. Kennedy in the White House*. Boston: Houghton Mifflin, 1965.

THE NATIONAL SECURITY ARCHIVES. The Cuban Missile Crisis, 1962. Vol 1. Project Editor Laurence Chang. Alexandria: Chadwyck-Healy, Inc., 1990.

The Washington Post, Sunday May 2, 1976.

TORREIRA CRESPO, RAMÓN and JOSÉ BUAJASÁN MARRAWI. *Operación Peter Pan. Un caso de Guerra psicológica* [Operation Peter Pan: A Case of Psywar]. Havana: Editora Política, 2000.

U.S. CONGRESS. SENATE. *Alleged Assassinations Plots Involving Foreign Leaders: an Interim Report of the Select Committee to Study Governmental Operations with Respect to Intelligence Activities*. 94th Cong., 2d sess., Report No. 94-465, Vol 1. Washington D.C.: U.S. Government Printing Office, 1975.

U.S. DEPARTMENT OF STATE. *Foreign Relations of the United States, 1961-1963,* Vol 10, *Cuba 1961-1962*. Washington D.C.: U.S. Government Printing Office, 1997.

VALDÉS-DAPENA, JACINTO. "El Programa de multiple vía" [The Multi-track Program]. Research report. CIHSE, Havana, 1996.

WASSILSEIV, W. N. et al. *Geheimnisse der USA. Geheimdienst*. Berlin: Deutscher Verlag del Wissenschaften, 1975.

RELEASED PAPERS

Presented at a Conference of scholars, former officials from the Kennedy administration, White House, CIA and State Department, and former members of the anti-Castro Resistance: "The Bay of Pigs: New Evidence from Documents and Testimony of the Kennedy Administration, the Anti-Castro Resistance and Brigade 2506," held in Musgrove Plantation, St. Simons Island, Georgia, May 31 – June 2, 1996:

National Security Council Meeting. Saturday, April 22, 1961.
Memorandum for the Record. First Meeting of General Taylor's Board of Inquiry on Cuban Operations Conducted by CIA. April 23, 1961.

Memorandum, Ultrasensitive, Memorandum for the Record at the Conference Room (214). Director of Central Intelligence Agency at 1350, April 24, 1961.

Memorandum from the President's Special Assistant (Schlesinger) to the Political Warfare Sub Committee of the Cuban Task Force. Washington. May 1, 1961.

Memorandum: Reactions to Cuba in Western Europe. Arthur Schlesinger Jr. to President Kennedy. May 3, 1961.

Cuba Study Group. Memorandum, Conclusions of the Cuba Study Group. June 13, 1961.

Cuba Study Group. Seminary: Immediate Causes of the Failure of Operation Zapata. June 13, 1961.

Memorandum from the President's Special Assistant (Schlesinger) to the President Assistant Special Counsel (Goodwin). Washington, July 8, 1961.

Memorandum for the Record by the Chief of Naval Operations (Burke). Washington, July 26, 1961.

Memorandum for the Record by Robert Kormer of the National Security Council Staff. Washington, August 16, 1961.

Memorandum for the President. August 22, 1961.

Memorandum for the President's Assistant Special Counsel (Goodwin) to the President Kennedy. Washington, November 1, 1961.

Memorandum to the Secretary of State, the Secretary of Defense, the Director of the CIA, the Attorney General, General Taylor, General Landsdale, Richard Goodwin. November 30, 1961.

Draft 11.1.61. Cuba Program Review by Brig. General Edward G. Landsdale. Chief of Operations. The Project. 18 January, 1962.

Guidelines for Operation Mongoose. 14 March 1962.

Memorandum for the Chief of Operations, Operation Mongoose. Covert Activities. 7 August, 1962.

Memorandum from the Department of Defense Operations Officer for Operation Mongoose (Craig) to the Special Group (Augmented). Washington, August 8, 1962.

Memorandum for the Director of Central Intelligence. August 8, 1962.

Memorandum of Meeting with President Kennedy, August 23, 1962. Central Intelligence Files.

Memorandum from the Chief of Operations, Operation Mongoose (Landsdale) to the Special Group (Augmented). Washington, September 12, 1962.

Counter-Revolutionary Handbook. October 10, 1962.

Memorandum for the Record. Subject: Mongoose Meeting with Attorney General, 16 October, 1962.

Naval War College, Review, Text of Lecture, Paramilitary Case Study. The Bay of Pigs, Lyman B. Kirkpatrick, Jr. Volume XXV. No. 2, November-December 1972.

Office of the Secretary of Defense. Washington 25, DC 23 July 1962.

Program Review by Brig. General Landsdale. The Cuba Project. 20 February 1962.

Record of Action by the National Security Council 478th Meeting, August 22, 1961.